SOME CONTEMPORARY NOVELISTS
(MEN)

SOME CONTEMPORARY NOVELISTS
(MEN)

BY
REGINALD BRIMLEY JOHNSON

Essay Index Reprint Series

originally published by
LEONARD PARSONS

 BOOKS FOR LIBRARIES PRESS
FREEPORT, NEW YORK

First Published 1922
Reprinted 1970

STANDARD BOOK NUMBER:
8369-1521-6

LIBRARY OF CONGRESS CATALOG CARD NUMBER:
77-107719

PRINTED IN THE UNITED STATES OF AMERICA

INTRODUCTION

IT is obviously always dangerous, if not impossible, to group any number of original writers without prejudice or injustice. The label so often misses the true significance of their work in any attempt to adjust it with our preconceived ideas. Yet the novelist must be—more probably than the poet, critic, or philosopher—susceptible to the trend of thought in his own day, more observant of contemporary events, habits, and social conditions. Where the material, or atmosphere, is identical, there will be common factors in the work. The critic, again, must consider all work in relation to the past, comparing the volumes he has to estimate with those from times already tested by history; put in their place, as it were, by the verdict of posterity.

There can, surely, be no question that in the years immediately preceding our own, serious novelists were mainly influenced by what may be called the Gissing realism, the literary expression of social revolt and moral scepticism, which prided itself upon the ruthless exposure of cant, leaving no social or moral sore uncovered. It demanded, with some noise and much bustle, the most frank investigation of all conventional subterfuge, the full discussion of all established ethics. It screamed at Mrs Grundy, kicked the complacent suburban, and told the truth!

Above all, seizing an obvious weapon, it concentrated and expatiated upon the hidden problems of sex, those elemental forces of nature which touch the highest spiritual, and lowest physical, needs of man.

Mr W. L. George clearly presents the most confirmed exponent of this fiction-form. He has, moreover, as a critic proclaimed his adherence to the School. He has firmly declared that it is his right, nay, his duty, as a novelist, to expose cant, denounce hypocrisy, question authority—whether human or divine—and, in particular, to accentuate certain questions once held unbecoming a novelist; just as, in his judgment, they predominate over life. A novelist, he says, is the showman of life; one who is therefore bound to accurate and complete reproduction. Only a few personal and political convictions, very passionately sincere, carry his work out of the groove. He will not, like the extreme realist, merely observe and record: he must expound, preach, and denounce.

Most certainly, working on broadly similar lines, under what may, for convenience, be summarised as the Gissing influence, we have Mr Gilbert Cannan, Mr Hugh Walpole, Mr J. D. Beresford, and Mr D. H. Lawrence.

There was a time, indeed, when we looked for leadership to Mr Cannan. He entered the arena so well-equipped, so assured—it would seem—of his own powers and position, touched such vital issues from such original points of view. But he appears, in some way, to have lost grip on himself: he has not developed, achieved aim or direction, composed his output to any coherence or form. He does not know where he is, what he wants to say. Sometimes I doubt whether he is really at ease in the fetters of realism, which he wrapped around him in his infancy. The manner of it has captured his pen, maybe to his soul's destroying. There are times when romance peeps out among the dust-bins; we meet strange phrases in strange tongues. He has moments of spiritual idealism, sternly repressed for the most part, though they will out. Almost, I like to fancy, he understands love —apart from passion; sometimes he seems to lead us among the stars. It is perhaps a trivial detail, yet not surely without significance, that he clearly prefers the conventional, so-called happy, ending; which is. after all, frequently true to life.

Still the great bulk of his work, which is rather massive, burying these glimpses of shy ecstasy, is built on literal observation, deep in the muddy backwaters of human nature.

On the other hand, I know there are those who will not admit that Mr Hugh Walpole is, properly speaking, ever a realist at all. They claim, rightly enough, that he can—and does—construct a dramatic, completed tale; that he exalts genuine, romantic emotion; that he recognises the spiritual, and does not grovel among self-dissected egomaniacs. Realism with him, indeed, is rather an atmosphere, or point of view, than a mechanical method. He carries it, too, into wider, more cleanly, fields. He does not mutter and mope. He achieves genuine characterisation, not mere surface-photography.

Yet he has not escaped the toils; most obviously, its influences dictate his choice of subjects: the two murder-studies, the three pictures of abnormal family pride and obstinacy, the Russian soul-tangle, the many amplitudes of self-conscious analysis, the strained pose. He is very much concerned with those who are wrapped

INTRODUCTION 9

up in themselves, examine their own deeds and emotions with endless curiosity; applying their half-digested conclusions to dogmas on human nature. In one word, he is always self-conscious.

There can be no question, however, about Mr Beresford. He positively revels in the minute, and crowds his pictures with indecisions. Such infinitesimal elaborations of tortured souls have never before been attempted, still less achieved. Devoutly, we hope, they may not direct the fashion. It is true that he carries realism beyond anything attempted by his literary godfathers. He works more beneath the surface than they. He does not determine, or define, character by the tilt of an eyelash. But he, too, gropes and fumbles among a thousand trivialities, never reaching results, so that his people remain unformed. He raises, with infinite patience, immense and tottering scaffoldings of a man's soul, but never reveals the building they were, surely, designed to support. Though he deals with emotions, he does not grasp them. He has, indeed, seen through the materialistic superficiality of the earlier realists; but he still observes, he does not feel or create. Nor, perversely, can he make up his own mind about any person or thing. Particularly in these most characteristic volumes which expound Jacob

Stahl, Mr Beresford sets down, not only a thousand passing, and really trivial, sayings and thoughts of his hero, but he shows us the man puzzling and wondering what he might have said had he been other than he was; what he really felt, or what he imagined he must feel. He gives us elaborate experiments in various versions, that none of them quite express his thought, or describe his emotions. It is, no doubt, a difficult matter to clothe thought or emotion in words; but the reader has no desire to wade through an author's search after the right phrase, to compare his various false starts. We look for results, the final, and best, form. Such records of careful endeavour may be honest, indeed, but they do not add the truth to the picture, they confuse the effect, and are, in themselves, somewhat tedious.

There are obvious characteristics in Mr D. H. Lawrence which would tempt one to dismiss his work as the last word in decadent realism. Holding the false gospel of Mr W. L. George that "life is most vivid when it is most unpleasant," he does certainly see "the dung-hill very well, and not at all the spreading chestnut tree above." In many parts of "The Lost Girl," and "The White Peacock," even in one lengthily analysed thought of "Sons and Lovers," and in all his later work, which has steadily deteriorated, he is " so excessive sexually as to seem repulsive." Everywhere he magnifies this aspect of truth into untruth; not with the courage of frankness, but with a morbid moral twist.

Yet when spontaneously himself and free from pose, Mr Lawrence could once rise to sincere art and the best instincts of romance. Whether in novels or verses, his nature-reading was always indeed of the senses without a soul, which sees the world " as a passionate allegory of human desire, human satisfaction, and human satiety." But he had vision. Nearer, perhaps, than any of his generation to Thomas Hardy; his characters did verily hold " communion with pure wild things, numberless, frail, and folded meekly in the evening light." Their souls were close to the " red and warm earth, the dark succulent green of blue-bell sheaths," the " grey-green clusters of spears and many white flowerets." He should learn, indeed, to detach Wagner and Verlaine from the pit's head and the plough; but George of " The White Peacock," the brooding Miriam of " Sons and Lovers," are true nature's children, clinging, through all the hard puzzle of life, to their mother's breast.

And if Mr Lawrence will over-emphasise the body, he can at times read the heart. Alvina Houghton makes many horrible false starts, quite inhuman; but the soul-mastery of Cicio is sincere and true. A real Lettie grew out of the opposed man-magnets with their finely adjusted appeal. Mrs Morel, and her rivals in Paul's heart, are very human and quite alive.

Mr Lawrence must learn to avoid emphasis and acquire ideas, not more moods. He has revealed true art, the creative gift, and the imaginative impulse.

So much for realism to-day. Against that influence towards decay we have Mr Snaith, who is, without qualification, a convinced romantic. He writes of his own age; his are characters we all know and might meet any day, yet they are not quite of this world. There is a glamour of the visionary on every page: not merely the romance form, but its most spiritual essence. Here are no half-measures: he does not even attempt to copy real life. We do not, indeed, find any stirring movement—the rush and rage of an old saga, the colour of stage costume, the heroism of the flashing sword. These are rather adventures of a man's soul; but they are none the less adventurous, conceived of the imagination, weaving their own romance. His heroes and heroines, be they gay maids or sad poets, are of the spirit world, wandering among men who have missed the vision, cannot hear the voice. Yet had we their faith or their fancy, saw we the meanings they see, we should be even as they. For all their wonderful thoughts, despite the unusual range of their experience, they are in themselves true to human nature, they are children of men. This is the real romance: the song of a man's soul; all we might be, and dream of being, which is so much greater and more beautiful than what we are. Mr Snaith is always vigorous, clear, and constructive. He has no use for false heroics or high-flown sentimentalism, but few writers have been more stimulating and suggestive.

There is something of the same spirit in Mr E. M. Forster, who has chosen, however, in part, to clothe his message in supernatural allegory, a sort of modern fairy-tale, which has its own charm and value, more subtly conveyed, but still with a meaning for man. Elsewhere he uses more normal material than Mr Snaith's, but sees it, also, with eyes awake to the ideal. He has produced but little, yet each tale, and all his characters, have individuality. Told with a light, easy touch, they provoke thought and excite interest.

There follows what one may call "stage" romance, in Mr John Buchan and Mr Neil Lyons. The former uses material adventure, the dangers and difficulties of travel in strange lands, the thrill of political intrigue, the colour of disguise, the rush of pursuit, the sound methods of a school always popular. He does his work rather particularly well. His equipment is quite complete.

Mr Lyons exploits London and the poor. He has a ready infectious wit, and all the *flaire* of a born journalist. He can be at once exact in costume, but fanciful in selection. These dear, good people speak very precisely as do the actual denizens of mean streets; but they are arranged and grouped with a keen eye to effect, artfully posed for the footlights. The work is 2d. coloured, and well worth the price.

A confirmed romantic, despite the over-accentuated modernity of his setting, we have Mr Compton Mackenzie, the fluent. It is true that, with the most copious wealth of detail, he uses the lens of a photographer. But he does not labour in the field. He romps there, for sheer joy, in the bright wonder of what he imagines to be the land of many and great sins. There is in him a fury of zest for the forbidden underworld, and he throws over it all the golden haze of his romantic fire, the mysticism of the idealist, moving unsullied among dark spirits, the modern Quixote, mad yet sublime. We are carried along, knee-deep in mud yet quite unsoiled, by the rushing sparkle of his tumultuous verbosity, the bright glitter of his lambent wit, his wealth of music in word and phrase. We forgive, or forget, the audacious falsity, the sham sentiment, for his untamable boy's heart. He does it all so well, with such complete abandon. We can realise that, after all, there is something here which is peculiarly his own, a genuine individuality he has really discovered for himself.

It does not appear, for instance, in the more normal " Passionate Elopement "—an old-fashioned romance, which many a poorer novelist could have conceived and written; while in the marvellous love-story of " Guy and Pauline," it reigns supreme. Mr Mackenzie's work is a unique example of the extreme manner and material of the realist, applied—with unbounded gusto—to the aroma of wild romance.

Mr Frank Swinnerton I have purposely left for a climax, that he may stand alone. For reasons it is not quite simple to estimate, I feel he has greater promise than any other of his contemporaries, and represents, more fully, with more assured power, the thought and hope of his generation. To begin with, one can judge him with more confidence, because he is, in the conventional sense, a more successful artist. In every volume he tells, briefly and dramatically, a finished tale, constructs a complete fiction, presents a group of clearly conceived characters. There is always atmosphere; varied, but neither wandering, hesitating, nor obscure. He gives us the finished product, nothing half-baked, undigested, or experimental. We do not see him observing or investigating, painfully and with effort; we enjoy the result of all he has seen and heard. He is realistic in the true sense of not fearing the truth; he is modern in the best sense of facing the difficulties, and in a measure the ugliness, of real life. But he creates like an artist: neither fearing his own vision, nor trusting to mere photography.

His is the voice of youth. He has all a boy's strength, confidence, and hope; not despising the riper wisdom which age and experience confer, not neglecting or belittling the deeper happiness which a courageous maturity may bring. He is yet of his own age, his own day. He has chosen, with all the vigorous sincerity of his alert mind, to reveal that special gift which youth has for the world: its vital curiosity, keen joy, rich hope, and inexhaustible power of recovery from disappointment and despair; its resolution to break chains; its resolve to achieve results. He believes in, and understands, the power of love. He has faith in a new world. He faces the problem of man's will towards himself and towards others, his diverse instincts and divided emotions, his sure sense of right and wrong. "Nocturne" is a supreme achievement of compressed art; every volume is an accomplished and workmanlike production.

All of which may sound extravagant, for Mr Swinnerton is not yet of the great masters. He has not the godlike immensity of George Meredith; neither the wealth of phrase nor the Olympian laughter of that giant genius, long and deeply matured to all the profundities of human nature. He has not the sixth nature-sense of Thomas Hardy, reading the riddle of Mother Earth. He has not the fine-spun subtlety of Henry James, that great citizen of the world.

But he has spoken for eternal youth, and is the greatest artist among his immediate contemporaries.

This generation, indeed, are alive, penetrating, and determined in high resolve. If, as we fear, some still let their feet trail in the muddy byways of their morbid immediate predecessors, they have a sincere longing for the real truth. They reflect, and vigorously express, what we are all puzzling over, perhaps despairing over, and yet—in our several degrees—eager to mend. They have their eyes upon better things. From novels like these, as from others of these years, we can read the hearts of our young men, understand their thoughts and their desires, forgive their anger, and rejoice in their hope.

Mr Walpole, indeed, in " The Young Enchanted " has given us an explanation of youth : which, if not final, is full of suggestive thought.

The war, he maintains, has brought us back " boys of eighteen chronologically supposed to be twenty-four." He says of London, " for the young, for everyone under thirty it's grand. There's a new city to be built, all the pieces of the old one lying around to teach you lessons—the greatest time to be born into in the world's history." His girl heroine declares that, when saying to herself she's perfectly miserable, " I'm not really, because there's something behind it all that I'm enjoying hugely. I wouldn't miss a moment of it. I want every scrap. It is *like* an enchantment really." In her earlier unclouded happiness the very bewilderment of other people fired her gaiety: " Everything's breaking up and everything's turning into new shapes and new colours. And I love it! I love it! I love it! I oughtn't to, it's wrong to. I can't help it . . . it's enchanting."

In one way this may be described as a clear message, but it does not, certainly, either inspire or penetrate all contemporary fiction, and scarcely helps us to determine what form the novel may take to-morrow; whether, in fact, it will yet awhile achieve any assured, settled position; wear any standard, defined, artistic form.

. . . . . .

It should, perhaps, be clearly explained that certain " great " writers are here omitted, just because they are *established* masters of fiction: H. G. Wells, J. M. Barrie, Conrad, and Arnold Bennett. Others, whose work is still vital and influential, have been too long with us to be—strictly—contemporary, and a few quite modern novelists, who are also dramatists, have been left for a later volume in this series.

Even so my selection may be condemned—in commission and omission; but such judgments and such criticism must be always arbitrary; must, in the last event, largely depend on temperament and taste.

The writers discussed here are all pre-eminently alive and of the immediate present; some scarcely known before the war. They present, I believe, the prevailing thoughts and chief literary vigour of our generation; if it be still rather a "promise" than a fulfilment. Theirs is to-day's work, pushing ajar, maybe, the door through which already we catch a glimpse of where we may one day reach, what we may one day mean.

Since completing the judgments here expressed, and the attempt to read therein a general atmosphere and point of view, I have found an interpretation, so similar as to justify a reference for support, of the New, spiritual Realism.

Like myself a Victorian who yet welcomes a freer and brighter youth, Mr Arthur Waugh[1] sharply compares the earlier "naturalist" revolt, from which romance was banished altogether, with the New Realism "of which romance is the very life blood."

"For the artist of the New Realism the kingdom of heaven lies within the soul of man; for the Realist of the last generation it was sought from without—in the general improvement of social and human conditions." His typecharacters were "not true to life at all."[2]

"Tradition and Change," 1919.

"We hail, then, in this latest development of English fiction a definite, sincere, and successful attempt to speak the truth about the things that belong to peace of the human soul. The New Realism goes straight to the heart of man and finds it of mingled yarn, good and ill together. . . . While it recognises the omnipotent claim of romance and true sentiment, it has banished sentimentality altogether from the stage." It is not "afraid of the naked beauty of pure passion," but the "ugly and gross are recognised at once as disgraceful."

So have I too read, here and in "Contemporary Novelists—Women," the New Realism.

R. BRIMLEY JOHNSON.

CONTENTS

	PAGE
INTRODUCTION	5
GILBERT CANNAN	25
HUGH WALPOLE	53
W. L. GEORGE	79
J. D. BERESFORD	97
D. H. LAWRENCE	121
COMPTON MACKENZIE	131
J. C. SNAITH	155
E. M. FORSTER	173
JOHN BUCHAN	183
NEIL LYONS	193
FRANK SWINNERTON	201

SOME CONTEMPORARY NOVELISTS

GILBERT CANNAN

THERE are moments when Mr Gilbert Cannan seems almost an idealist; he can certainly be tender with the simply good.

It is, most unexpectedly, in " Pink Roses " that we meet Ruth Hobday, and read how " Life is simple, life for man is contained in his friend and his love; two things—purity and power: and for a woman life is conception, first of her man, then of her child. . . . Home, love, a friend . . . these things lead to the unattainable." This is the true vision of romance—told also in " Young Ernest "—" all lovers should bring their love to the earth, and let the wind know it is there. How can you love in streets and houses ? "

There is a gentle and most attractive simplicity again which needs delicate handling in Francis Christopher Folyat, Bachelor of Divinity, and genuine Christian; a most unselfish loyalty in

Tibby M'Phail; generosity, very patient with ingratitude, in George Laurie. All three characters, of almost Biblical virtue, are revealed with sincere sympathy. But in his ordinary moods Mr Cannan alternates between cold and savage cynicism. " Marriage, killing each other in the first few weeks and then—humbug " is a definition that almost murders humanity by its off-hand brevity and callous restraint; whereas the violent phrasing of his tirade on " doing well"' in the world would be hard to match : " If a young man will lie, and sneak, and snivel, and kow-tow, and swallow his spittle, and gut his brains, tear out his heart, swear a fool's a genius, a knave an honest man, a wanton a pattern of purity, a journalist a poet, a tedious old man a miracle of wisdom, wit, and prudence —then, God help him, a young man can do marvels for himself."

It is his habitual humour to tilt at emotion and domesticities with a hard hand.

" It was too nearly the thing he wanted for him to let it go," thought Stephen; " a little pumping up—squeeze—there you are—warmth— the light in the eyes, and if that is not love, it is like enough. It will serve."

So had Matilda reduced " old Mole " " to that condition wherein men and women believe that never has the world been visited by such love, and that they will go on loving for ever and ever. This she achieved by leaving his affections to look after themselves, and concentrating herself on seeing that he was properly fed and clothed, had the requisite amount of sleep, and just enough cosseting to make him wish for more, which he did not get."

For herself, " ignorant, untaught, unprepared, love had been a kiss of the lips, a surrender to the flood of perilous feeling, a tampering with forces that might or might not sweep you to ruin : a matter of fancy, dalliance, and risk."

In a word, Society is not permanent. " Its existence depends entirely on its power to adapt itself to life. It is certainly independent of the innumerable sentimental ideas with which men endeavour to plaster up the cracks in its walls, among which I must count that of home. Home, I conceive, has a meaning for children. It is the place where they grow up. We make homes for our young as the birds make nests for theirs. When the children go forth then the home is empty and is no longer home." Again, " Men and women only make love to each other as a rule because they love each other so little that they've nothing else in common."

On the other hand, he is no less severe on civilisation and " industrial development which drives men to a frenzy so that they know not what they do." " There were no standards, neither of life nor of art. There could not be, for there was no time for valuation, just as there was no time for thinking. Here and there he found an ideal or two, but such wee, worn, weary little things, so long bandied about among brains that could not understand them and worried into decline by the shoddy rhetorical company they had been forced to keep. . . . He did not make the world, and he does not believe that he can undo anything, good or evil which, for the world's purposes, is necessary to be done."

I am a little surprised that Mr Cannan permits so many of his heroes to attain happiness. Mostly, indeed, they drift into intimacy with ladies like Cora of the " Pink Roses," who " kissed his eyes, his lips, his ears, and bit the tip of his nose until it was bruised and swollen," but having " never the smallest real intention of not taking up the life for which they were designed by birth, tradition, and circumstance," they are not submerged, but easily " drift out again." For them, finally, " marriage is life's great adventure. . . . If ever you find yourself faced with a risk, take it. Love, I conclude, is a voyager, and it is our privilege to travel with him; but if we stay too long in the inn of habit, we lose his company, and we are undone."

Mr Cannan, accepting the critic as a " policeman," declares that the " man of genius is a man who has the courage of his instinct for expression." Modern fiction he conceives of as begging us to " come inside and see what woman is like." What the average man cannot " stand about women is the way they go nosing round. . . . My sister does. *She wants to know how a man works.* She's like me with a motor." But " men are going to be very wonderful now.

They will force women to be truthful by understanding them."

On the whole, however, Mr Cannan is very much more keen about revealing character than about talking wisely upon the philosophy of life. He abhors the conventional, chiefly because he finds it supremely uninteresting. For him the man with a twist, or kink, in his nature has an invincible attraction. No one of his heroes is quite normal; all discover the adventure in life, waiting somewhere for every one of us. He is realistic in description, romantic in atmosphere. His the actual world around us, with its meaning revealed by imagination. He is concerned, not so much with what exists or happens, as with what man desires and intends to create and discover. He can idealise men and women while scorning their limitations and hating their environment. While lingering with, and denouncing, the stark senseless cruelty and ugliness of life, he admits sunshine everywhere.

Technically speaking, Mr Cannan is not a reformer. He tells his story and constructs his plot in the approved manner. But he has caught, in an acute form, the modern obsession for elaborate photography of childhood; he is largely dominated by sex, and though he does not indulge in sequels, the persons and places of his earlier stories reappear often in later volumes, between which there is no very marked differentiation to witness advance.

All these characteristics began early, and have never left him. " Peter Homunculus," the tale of one who suffers from being " infernally young," opens in a curiously similar atmosphere to that of Mr Snaith's " William Jordan, Junior," published two years earlier. It is, moreover, deliberately reminiscent of " Evan Harrington." But Mr Cannan certainly does not follow either Meredith or Mr Snaith. William Jordan remains a stranger among men, and his life has a rare completeness. Evan leaves us in perfect happiness, with a fair promise of great things.

To Peter's future we have no clue. As usual, Mr Cannan declines any conclusion; his besetting sin. Like so many a brother-hero, the boy aspires to authorship and publishes his first book on the last page. " After all, it is a trade," and, having spent his youth as a bookseller, one imagines he may succeed. But this favourite device of modern writers—to elaborate life's openings, and leave their hero upon its threshold —is scarcely satisfying, and may be criticised, without injustice, as shirking the real issue. The character here is only half made; youth not only suffers, but provides, illusions : the real test comes from how he turns out. The modernists have, somewhat perversely, gone back to old convention of leaving their heroes when marriageable, if unmarried. The taste for fiction—after the altar—seems to have suffered a decline.

We admit that Peter is an attractive young egoist, shrewd enough at the last to realise that " he is not a man, but an ass laden with books " —a " tiny man," son of a drunken tailor.

Phenomenally susceptible, and singularly

charming to all women, his social philosophy proves strangely disordered.

> " Does any man want any woman, or any woman any man? Are these wild flashes more than things of a moment? . . . Is not every woman any man's woman? Is not every man any woman's man? Why property? Why impossible pledges? Why pretend so much that is obviously false? Why build upon a lie and call it sacred? . . . Why do men and women live hideously together? . . . Why, and why again? "

To which the wise Wicksteed :

> " Them sort of men that are always waggin' their tongues about life in general nearly always come to grief. . . . That's what I calls being in love, when you're grovellin' to the woman one moment, an' spittin' in 'er face the next. In the books it's all grovellin'."

Certainly Mattie Scott spoiled Peter, with her noble and frank girlhood; so did the " glorious " Mary Douglas, with her tragic experience of life. Besides, there was dear Mrs Crewe, the great Wilson, and old Cooper; not to name Tessa and " Evening Glory Jane." Youth can absorb so much : colouring and turning it all to his own glory, the uplifting or the undoing of his almighty self. And, despite his " absurd introspective habit," the opening of " Peter's career," as here told, has immense interest. Mr Cannan has entered into every detail with such genuine gusto, and much complete understanding,

He is Youth to-day, as was "Pendennis" of the Victorians. "You see," he declares, with fascinating *naïveté*, "I know myself, and I know exactly where I shall go wrong."

In one mood he can dismiss all women as "liars and web-spinners; webs to catch worthless flies," but another reveals woman—"if she is cruel I must accept as I would the cruelty of the earth, or the wind, or the sea."

Yet, in the end, he learnt that if "women are an infernal nuisance, without them nothing is done," and that "there is no more blazing folly than for the man to dictate, for in all matters of love the instinct of the woman is true."

"Devious Ways," again, published ten years ago, is a work of expert maturity. David Brockman is not Renè Fourny ("Young Ernest") in embryo, but his twin—with a difference, and again bears considerable similarity to Serge Folyot in "Round the Corner." Character and circumstances are similar in all three. David is driven from home by a horrible stepmother; Renè by a bad father, who, however, has charm; Serge from the need for a larger life, and the incompetence of both his parents. Renè achieves experience in a London mews; Serge and David from travel into the far corners of the earth. To the end Serge remains self-sufficient, fathering the responsibilities of his family, seeking no mate; David and Renè marry for romance.

There is, perhaps, rather more crudity in Mr Cannan's picture of David's family than the others. Mrs Brockman is almost a stage type:

harsh, domineering, and intolerant, making her husband's fortune at the expense of his soul. She would antagonise any young man. There is, too, a certain vagueness about David's experience in the Colonies and America, while the persons more clearly drawn are melodramatic. The quixoticism of his chivalrous attitude towards Nina, and her mother's suicide, suggest the Adelphi. The elder lady, you see, had an unwholesome notoriety her daughter could scarcely escape, and she was better dead.

And though David, incidentally, champions other " distressed females," he is far from a perfect knight. There is a married lady to whom, for no reason very apparent to the reader, he is temporarily attracted, wherefore he finds heaven only by " devious ways." Nina, forgiving, " thinks she never loved him till then. . . . There was so much that I did not know "—a frank but curious attitude towards infidelity.

But the most unsatisfying figure here remains " the boyish vision of Helen." She had, indeed, been the guardian angel of David's boyhood; never, I suspect, really loving another; and, without doubt, helping and guiding his young brothers and sisters left at home. Yet we are told she made an unhappy marriage and, after that tragic adventure, returned to her father's house, alone, but not a widow. The real inwardness of character is not even indicated, and we have absolutely no clue as to the nature of her tragedy. Yet in the early chapters she is the centre of the picture.

C

Serge is himself more vaguely outlined, less realised; his family far more finished and individual. The Reverend Francis, indeed, has some claim to be reckoned the real hero of the story. There are few characters in fiction revealing such genuine Christianity, combined with moral weakness and want of backbone. Yet he could, and did, fight those who blasphemed him—after his own fashion, indeed, but with singular courage and dignity, proving the victor. His touching, half-humorous, and quite unclerical sympathy with the vulgar depravity of Frederick shows most original subtlety; and in the most difficult duties of a father he never fails. There was no help here from his wife who "regarded her destiny as a thing that happened automatically, for she was in mind a child, and life was to her a toy presented to her by a beneficent creator, already wound up and prepared to go on indefinitely." Only a saint could love such a woman.

Finally, for Renè life has scarcely a meaning outside love, or rather, sex. In childhood he is nearly absorbed by almost passionate devotion, in vain seeking complete understanding, for the mother whose life had been wrecked by marrying the wrong man; yet he is "wonderfully in love"; wholly subject, when with his Cathleen, to a romantic enchantment as he "prepares for her a couch of bracken." We are led, however, to suppose this beautiful vision merely an episode, as Cathleen entirely vanishes after the opening chapters; and Renè succumbs to the shrewd

Linda, who, recognising his unusual brainpower, determines to make him a great man, and share, as his wife, the excitement of leadership in an intellectual and artistic atmosphere. She is brilliant and quick-witted, though quite superficial, and astoundingly insincere, with the inevitable result that, after marriage, Renè not only sees through her attractions, but learns to detest her manœuvring on his behalf. Intellectually he has no ambition : he will not climb.

They separate, practically by mutual consent, and he simply drifts to London, wandering through crowded thoroughfares, utterly without aim or object. Being the man he is, we cannot marvel to find him soon established at Mitcham Mews, number 6, with the delightful Ann Pidduck—a true Cockney, also a true woman. Mr Cannan has devoted much care to the drawing of this naïve, and yet shrewd, young person : amply justifying his labour. She is, to my mind, one of the most charming and original characters in fiction, for whose final despair our hearts bleed. And, for her, he has no cynicism, no false subtlety. She is thoroughly vivid and alive; loyal, passionate, and straight; the best of comrades, and in no way posed.

Unfortunately Renè, for all his powers of sympathy with free and simple humanity, is an essentially modern young creature, fond of *any* experience, but—in the end—seeking the complex. Wherefore Ann again proves unsatisfying, and with a strange hovering of romance,

Mr Cannan quite unexpectedly re-discovers his Cathleen and, after a few chapters of unadulterated super-analysed realism, brings the lovers to the " sweet comfort " of " being together " once more.

Accepting, in the same spirit as Nina, the man's conception of his duty " to keep the flame alight in woman," she is terrified sometimes to realise " how near she came to being one of his failures." It was, indeed, only a narrow escape they had from " sleep and death." Though given to drifting he was just " earnest " enough for ultimate victory. As a less strenuous friend put it, " We live in a world of women, my boy, and we must make the best of it."

When Mr Cannan wrote " Little Brother," I presume he had in the back of his mind the intention to portray genius, as so many of his contemporaries have attempted. The title subtly conveys the attitude of his narrative, which, in this case, is told by the hero's sympathetic, but more Philistine, elder brother, who loves and admires, even while cursing, the erratic Stephen : himself a Laurie, as were also the " Three Pretty Men," created four years later. They are a dour family, and our genius had even more rough edges than all the rest. He is, in fact, almost inhuman in personal relationships; a ferocious egotist; utterly without gratitude and, though hyper-sensitive and given to wild enthusiasm, quite inconstant and faithless. He achieves nothing, and can be depended upon for nothing by anyone. Not an attractive personality, you will say. Yet he was always ready for love, charmed many to devotion under the most trying circumstances, evinces genuine modesty, and—on occasion—worshipped an utter charlatan.

Mr Cannan, indeed, has introduced here a writer of enormous popularity, one Wherry, who created a type of fiction responsible for a certain sticky sentimentality in the English mind which, though not quite clearly analysed, stands for something in literature which excites his unmitigated contempt. That Stephen was taken in by such patent insincerity and blatantly false art, argues a serious flaw in his critical acumen which no doubt helps to account for his own failure. On the other hand quite other characteristics caused his breaking away from the patient and generous George, who took him to Cambridge, paid all his bills, and generally fathered the lad, always suffering his incredible impertinence: the fact being that older men, notably his own grandfather, understood and liked Stephen, simply because age, envying, is always tolerant of excess in youth.

As it is written in " Young Ernest," " no artist takes personal relationships seriously. They happen," although in Stephen, " one of those children grown up by mistake," the artistic instinct was less fully developed than the dramatic, which " seems to consist in throwing out a rope from yourself to someone else, and then pulling it tight until the other person begins to be afraid of falling; then you rock on your feet, and look down your nose, and fling the rope back."

Love, indeed, figures dramatically, though without dignity, in his life, and certainly injures his work. His engagement to Miss Wherry, with her bright, hard egotism, prolongs his blindness towards the hypocrisy of her father—though, ultimately, the occasion of rupture: his philandering with Miss Laxton blunts his critical judgment: and the ultimate union with Alison, the primitive maid-servant whom he had loved in boyhood, does not promise comradeship with an intellectual equal. Mr Cannan, indeed, rather shirks the psychology of this conclusion. Still, Alison has personality, and, if she accepts immorality as inevitable, it has not killed the essential womanliness of her nature. After all, maybe in her we can recognise those primal qualities which the best in man, that is the most instinctive or natural, needs in his mate.

The Caledonian philosopher who advised Stephen, " Never tell the truth to an Englishman; it hurts him," might have been writing the motto for " Three Pretty Men." This is the Epic of an Invasion—from Scotland into that industrial purgatory of industrialism, the mean-spirited, bustling, and self-centred town of Thrigsby in which so many of Mr Cannan's heroes are doomed to dwell. The Lauries, like their countrymen under James I., are poor but proud. There is no limit to their confidence in themselves. They will absorb and annex

England. Only for each, the aim and the ambition differ in detail, actually producing perpetual conflict between themselves. The mother and her three sons have only one common quality; the conviction of superiority. She would follow, without hesitation, the line marked out by earlier invaders, elders of her own clan, " warm " men, leaders in town and trade, prospering on English gold. She desires, and expects, them to welcome her sons, give the boys a good start, make their fortunes. This, in fact, is the policy actually adopted by one " Pretty Man." Brother Tom carries out the instructions of Mrs Laurie to the letter. He is satisfied with the result, amply rewarded by success. Only ignoring the wider vision of Mrs Laurie, thinking throughout in terms of Thrigsby, scorning her dreams of *real* greatness; he is a spiritual failure, a moral pygmy. John proves even more of a puzzle, less satisfying. From the beginning he would owe nothing to rich relatives. He must make his own way, which, on the other hand, does not lead to any distinguished position, any leadership among men. His aim is not the conquest of others, but modest competence, personal freedom, and reasonable comfort for himself. He seems, all the time, a little outside family life and the home. Affectionate, loyal, and above all— straight; his conception of sonship and brotherhood remains always subservient to independence and common sense.

The main interest, however, centres about

Jamie, who, the first to leave Scotland, bearing the soul shock of the alien, never himself grows acclimatised to the soil he prepares for others. He is, like so many of Mr Cannan's heroes, always a stranger among men; constantly kicking against the conventions and respectability. Super-sensitive to the general opinion he holds in scorn, tender and chivalrous towards failure or loneliness, he must be always fighting his own battle in life, never confident of victory. He finds men cruel, morals chaotic. Again and again flushed by the vision of new ideals; yet seeing no end beyond what facts and experience force him to call an illusion. Superficially ineffective, he is the constant rebel, his millennium in the clouds.

Always "the change in him was sudden and violent . . . everything was a puzzle to him. . . . Mutual understanding seems to him so rare and high a mystery that it was not to be looked for in common life."

He had never found understanding in love. As a youth attracted by the stage-struck daughter of a clerk in his uncle's office, who rewarded his generosity by running away with a boy dramatist; he learned to worship a gracious vision of noble and brilliant womanhood, who threw herself away upon the vulgar stability of his brother Tom. Only the luckless Tibby—maid of all work and yet loyal friend to the family—the "poor relation" immortalised, really followed his moods and gave him true sympathy. Shrewd, strong, and sympathetic;

of startling audacity while always "knowing her place," she really supports the whole burden and responsibility of his life. Indeed, the realities of life for all ultimately depend on her, who was destined always to self-effacement, since, with the usual perversity of the male, even Jamie never fully acknowledged her sway.

Mr Cannan, in fact, makes no attempt to mature his hero. The closing page reaches no further than one more "passionate hope," as "he told himself he was sailing towards the new world where there had been Wars of Liberty."

There is new ground, viewed from a different angle, in "Old Mole," who may be taken for a life-size portrait of the sketch (in "Little Brother") called George. There is much here, more directly parallel than anything found in the other novels, to the usual interests of modern fiction.

We have, in the first place, very vivid impressions of school life as it affects the masters; in the second, a record of the soul awakened in middle-life; finally, sacrifice and effacement of age at the bidding of youth. Mr Cannan, moreover, has here indulged in many bitter, but scarcely exaggerated, generalisations upon art, literature, civilisation, and drama, which are the accepted hunting ground of contemporary novelists.

For Herbert Jocelyn Beenham (commonly called "Old Mole") was "foolishly, a little arrogantly, seeking in life the imaginative force, the mastery of ideas and human thoughts and feelings that he had found in literature. Life, maybe, proceeds through eruption and epidemic; art through human understanding, sympathy and will. . . . There were then three things: living, life, and art."

More incidentally, the pantomime reflects English character. It " is heavy, solid, gross, over coloured, disconnected, illogical, and unimaginative. On the other hand it is humorous, discreetly sensual, varied, and full of activity." It is cinemas which are ruining the country; as industrialism " drives men to frenzy, so that they know not what to do." While, as we read in " Pink Roses," the " appointed end of everything in modern England is music-hall government, music-hall newspapers, music-hall art, music-hall finance." Here, again, is the popular actress on serious intellectual drama: " There are no scenes in it. Nothing you can take hold of. I say my lines: the other people in the play don't seem to take any notice of them, but just go on talking. I suppose it's very clever, but it's not acting."

Old Mole himself liked to imagine after what fashion the two schools of playwright (the Intellectual and the Commercial) would dramatise the story of his life:

> " In the one it would be measured by rule of thumb, the eternal triangle, haloed husband, weeping wife, discomfited lover, or, if violent effects were sought for, the woman damned to an unending fall, the two men stormily thanking their vain and

shallow God they were rid of her; in the other it would be talked out of court, husband and wife would never rise above a snarl, and lover would go on talking; in both, men and women would be cut and trimmed to fit in with a formula. In the one, the equation would be worked out pat, in the other it would go sprawling on and on like the algebraic muddle of a flurried candidate in an examination who has omitted an x, and gone on in desperate hope of a result."

There is, I fear, somewhat similar " sprawling " and " going on talking " in modern fiction, among novelists seeking a definition of life in terms of art.

The Mole had " for twenty-five years slumbered away in an ancient and honourable profession, teaching awkward, conceited, and for the most part grubby little boys " what they quickly forgot. Despite his startling descent into Bohemia, he never quite shakes off the pedagogue. When events or persons prove puzzling, he must always reconcile them to some orderly conception of human nature: then " having fished out a theory, as he thought, to meet the case, he was quite content and prepared, untroubled, to enjoy his happiness."

Suddenly banished from the respectable placidity of his own world, the man is flung pell-mell into the very dregs of humanity, where all is primitive, lawless, and sordid. Only the girl Matilda, innocent cause of his downfall, stands out from the noisy crowd; just because she is not content, has ambitions, and—given her opportunity—the power to realise them. When, in fact, as his wife, she (again almost by accident) achieves phenomenal popularity, she does *not*, like other women, " cease to be anything but views and opinions and clothes." Loving luxury, and dependent upon constant change and excitement, she yet has real enthusiasm for her work; a curiously unformed, wholly instinctive, but quite real, interest in dramatic art. For his infinite generosity, tolerance, and admiration she shows at once profound respect and the tenderest affection, only a " dread that the comfort of such days could not last."

Her influence upon him is in one way simpler, in another, more subtle. Enjoying the wider experience involved in her success, the man grows gradually more and more content with love, his age learning to live in her youth. With no illusions, no personal hopes or ambitions, he is perfectly happy.

Not, perhaps, a healthy or natural state of mind. Mr Cannan, at any rate, will not allow his hero the uninterrupted possession of content. Feeling his young wife needs young society, he encourages her to make a great friend of one of his favourite pupils—with the inevitable result.

After a stormy interval of protest, the old man readily " shrank into the shadow," watching these two who did not see him. " You saw nothing but her," he writes, " and she saw nothing but you, and it was clear to me that you were enjoying your tenth honeymoon, which is surely a far greater thing than the first, if only you can get to it. . . . Are there children? I hope there are children. . . . There are two clear ideas in my head, and they desire each other in marriage—the idea of children and the idea of the theatre. . . . With this, I shake you by the hand and we three puppets dance on through the merry burlesque which our modern life will seem to the wiser and healthier generations who shall come after us."

To the last he remains tolerant, philosophical, optimistic : holding the great adventure of Love worth the risk.

It is a powerful story; full of interest in its general plot and narrative incidents; its subtle characterisation; its reflections on life and art.

One could scarcely imagine an atmosphere more vividly contrasted thereto than that of "Pink Roses." This is a mere study in sex, which seems to occupy (as Mr W. L. George claims for real life) more than nine-tenths of the story; and is far more prominent than in any other of his novels, except perhaps "Young Ernest." In this case Mr Cannan throws the blame, or the responsibility, upon the war.

Trevor Mathew was "left out" of things— through a weak heart. He could not, with his friends, go to the front; scholarship, art, or literature, all pursuits leading to mere culture, seem an impertinence : and, thrown off the rails, he drifts into emotionalism. A champion of primitive woman against censorious convention, he enters into a passionate partnership with Cora of the Pink Roses : the eternal feminine, born to dazzle and devour man. There are here, however, certain features of comradeship which are exceptional. She imagines, at any rate, that the arrangement may be permanent—" if you'd only make up your mind what you want to do, we could get married and go ahead." But " the thought of marriage had never crossed his mind." Which, however, does not imply indifference or hard-heartedness. His aim was to develop in Cora the ambition " to do something for its own sake and simply because you like it, not because you think I like it." He does, actually, secure for her the influence required for success on the stage; draws round her a large circle of gay and congenial friends, actors, and playwrights; and then, with no kind of explanation, simply withdraws himself from her life. He has no sense of desertion in so doing; and we do not believe she was unhappy. Simply, " he knew now what way he was going."

The decision of so complete a return to his own life was, no doubt, materially assisted by his growing devotion to Ruth Hobday, who represented Woman in purer altitudes. Under her influence he sees that " Life was simple. Life for man was contained in his friend and his love, two things, purity and power, and for a woman, life was conception, first of her man, then of her child. Home, love, a friend . . . these things led to the unattainable . . . So good-bye, good-bye, pink roses."

With her, he will once more resume his place, nobler and freer than the old avenues from which war uprooted him.

"We know all the things that people like my father have pretended not to know. . . . They wanted us to live the old life, but we could not do it because of each other. . . . Love has to begin again every time, at the beginning, in the world as it is and as it will be." And she thinks "men are going to be very wonderful now. They will just force women to be truthful by understanding them."

After all, even here, sex is *not* the end.

Mr Cannan, indeed, has contributed another disjointed effort towards the philosophy of War in that curious little "Book of Fables" entitled "Windmills," which, at moments, recalls Swift. Here we meet those who "had long ago arrived at the conclusion that there was no God, no ascertainable purpose in the universe, and nothing in life but the fun or the nuisance of living . . . if you can see the humour of your position, you can be happy and glad that you have lived." Women, we learn, "are the criminals who are responsible for everything, for they encourage men in their vanity and weaken them in their power." The wise man "spends his days looking for the devil," crying "Let us no longer be separate, but let us, man, woman, God, and devil, join together to bring forth joy, for until there is joy on earth there shall not be justice, nor kindness, nor understanding, nor any good thing."

This is more subtle than convincing, and, quite frankly, I find Mr Cannan's elaborate picture of the world ruled by woman both confusing and repulsive. He does not, I think, quite know where he is going, or what it concerns him to prove.

Mr Cannan lately published "the first of a series of books dealing with the chaos revealed by the War of 1914, and the Peace of 1919 . . . to discover the light thrown upon human nature by abnormal events and conditions." Unfortunately, upon these complex issues the author's own mind remains chaotic. To him, all wars "are just the same silly business, getting drunk before you go and when you come back, and saying nothing about what happened in between." There can be no Peace while a "town grows out of robbery, nothing but robbery, and some towns grow so big that they can rob whole countries." If "every man who owned more than one room for each member of his family" were "taken out and shot . . . there'd be a different story to tell."

Mr Cannan, indeed, has no more patience with "bleating" pacifists than with the most arrant jingo: "It's a poor sort of conscience that makes you change your furniture and your clothes and put up Shaw and Wells and Sidney Webb instead of Kitchener and Roberts and the King. They all look alike to me, for there is no difference between doing silly things and saying silly things."

That shrewd philosopher and hero, Dr Melian Stokes, is driven to hopeless brain-riot in his "pilgrim's progress" among modern men. He can neither hear nor see clearly amidst "the present din and confusion "; though " possessed by a torrential passion of elucidation," he leaves everything obscure. We can extract from this " dangerous eloquence " neither reasoned criticism nor a hint of truth. We " hear only words, words, words." Even youth, whom—like Old Mole—he had always worshipped, would " produce chaos wherever it went, the chaos that is the beginning of creation "—a somewhat comfortless optimism.

Mr Cannan, perhaps, would make no pretensions: he is content to be as muddled as the times we live in, and write novels like those Dr Stokes found so tasteless: " The form, the endless conversations, the casual psychology, the distortions necessary to make both ends meet seemed to him rococo and insipid. They were so cautious and indirect, so lacking in frankness, above all, in character, and therefore in style."

Surely modernity has written its own epitaph. That is " Pugs and Peacocks " to the life. Buried within this lumbering shapelessness there are certainly a few admirable character-sketches and brilliant descriptive paragraphs. " I'm not a liar," declares the fascinating Sharples, " if I am a lawyer." He had no " *reasoned* objection " to " going with the other fellows, like sheep, through a gap." It was " only a fence " conscience wouldn't allow him to take. Sharples is worth knowing. So is Hedwig of the " large olive face," who " had just enough house, just enough husband, just enough baby, just enough education and ideas . . . a very strict and satisfying economy "; to whose more luxurious brother-in-law (maker of buttons) the " presence of pretty girls was a digestive."

There is, indeed, on almost the last page of " Pugs and Peacocks " a " definition of something new . . . the prime psychological fact of the moment," found " in a young woman concentrated upon the logic of the situation." She has made " nonsense of the existing social system, developed a faculty in which men are lacking," that will create in men a " constructive capacity." " Which is all clear enough "—to Mr Cannan. Earlier, indeed, he states another aspect of modernity with greater clearness: the need for " an intelligent appreciation of the new dynamic rhythm " that has " broken through the old; the only rhythm to which men now respond, that of machinery, which, for all we know, may be nearer to the rhythm of life than anything men have been able to refine out of their emotions. In modern life there is nothing " beyond an " accomplished fact, the mass that move, work, eat, sleep to the sound of a hooter or a bell." Is there, in fact, room in the world for souls and the machine? To-day humanity stands in grave peril—of destruction by the engineer.

In fact, the final impression of these novels as a whole is a destructive negation. We all recognise that exceptional people, with whom he always busies himself, do not often make a success of life, judged by convention. But they do achieve: they possess personality. Now Mr Cannan's heroes are nearly all wanting in backbone. They are left striving for something they cannot accomplish, worrying about their own, unstable, ideals. Their moral force strikes out in a thousand directions, aiming nowhere. More often than we should expect they marry happily in the end, a conventional close to fiction : but, even then, they remain ineffective, almost formless. The characters he seems most to admire have many excellent qualities; but they remain undisciplined, incoherent; buildings set up without an architect.

Whether or not, as Mr Cannan would no doubt maintain, the limitation is, in fact, demanded by realism to actual life; it cannot prevent our unqualified admiration for the work. If, as we feel, there is occasional repetition of theme and atmosphere, Mr Cannan reveals remarkable strength and insight. Judged by the most old-fashioned standards he is always readable, that is by an absorbing narrative, firm—original— characterisation, and the dramatic instinct. He observes, reflects, and does not despise the ideal. Somewhat remorseless, a little cynical, and often brutally outspoken, yet he reveals faith in happiness and beauty. For him, ultimately, the adventure counts, the highest spirituality conquers, and is worth while.

PETER HOMUNCULUS	1909
DEVIOUS WAYS	1911
LITTLE BROTHER	1912
ROUND THE CORNER	1913
OLD MOLE	1914
YOUNG ERNEST	1915

52 SOME CONTEMPORARY NOVELISTS

WINDMILLS	1915
THREE PRETTY MEN	1916
EVERYBODY'S HUSBAND	1917
MUMMERY	1918
THE STUCCO HOUSE	1918
PINK ROSES	1919
PUGS AND PEACOCKS	1922

HUGH WALPOLE

"The secret of the mystery of life," says Mr Hugh Walpole, "is the isolation that separates every man from his fellow—the secret of dissatisfaction too, and the only purpose of life is to realise that isolation and to love one's fellow-man because of it, and to show one's courage like a flag to which other travellers may wave their answer."

It was this separating isolation we found a favourite theme of contemporary women novelists, whereby, at risk of egoism, they passionately seek Truth, "Truth to oneself"—the one thing, as he too declares, that really matters. They would not admit, indeed, Mr Walpole's almost opposing conclusion, "It's no use trying to keep out of things. As soon as they want to put you in—you're in. The moment you're born you're done for."

In other words he, at least, cannot stand aside; so that we find his work, however permeated with his own questionings and emotions, full of the problems that, after all, matter so much more to us than anything else in the world—our relations with our fellows, in so far closely allied to conventional fiction, constructed upon an orderly plot and the drama of man.

Mr W. L. George, indeed, claims that " Traill is the simple, delicate, and passionate young man that Mr Walpole would like to be, and that if ' The Prelude to Adventure ' is so very much his life in Cambridge, ' Mr Perrin and Mr Traill ' his career in a little school, ' Fortitude ' his life under the influence of London's personality —in ' Maradick at Forty ' he has attempted to make copy of his future." In fact he observes autobiographically. To Mr Walpole, indeed, life is always and pre-eminently an adventure : his hero is an explorer travelling ever with his life in his hands, " and as for the cruel selfishness of love, it's worth it. Life isn't life without it. Don't play for safety; it is the most dangerous thing in the world." Though " the whole duty of art is listening for the voice of God," in practice Mr Walpole accepts the dictum of his own Maurice Garden : " people don't want to know what a young ass thinks about life if he can't tell a story."

He has told many exciting and quite admirable stories.

Like a large number of our contemporary writers, Mr Walpole seems to have been born mature. " The Wooden Horse " of 1909 is even more assured than much of his later work, and quite as convincing. The tyrannical family atmosphere and tradition, like that overshadowing " The Duchess of Wrexe " and " The Green Mirror," is most dramatically opposed to that mastery of place over mind, reaching its climax in Cornwall, of which "Maradick at Forty" reveals the kindly, and "Fortitude" the sinister, power. We have here, indeed, much of the material for fiction, already handled without fumbling, from which Mr Walpole creates character, the favourite subjects of his art.

Henry Trojan, colonial ("The Wooden Horse"), is surely the spiritual father of Philip Mark, after years abroad bursting, with most unwelcome modernity and simple sentiment, upon a singularly stiff-necked family group. His son Robin, locked up and wedged by his proud, narrow-minded aunt and uncle, closely resembles young Henry of the House of Trenchard. It is Harry's to re-enter and to annex the home from which he had been banished in boyhood for some trivial defiance of parental authority. After his many years' dreams of passionate devotion to the place and the people, he finds everything changed, hostile, and suspicious. Chiefly his son Robin treats him contemptuously, scarcely with tolerance, as a rank outsider—ill-mannered, uncultured, blatant, and sentimental.

Here is dramatic material for domestic tragedy which can only be averted by something closely resembling the heroics of romance. Harry Trojan, indeed, is a figure of chivalry— to every man, woman, and child of his acquaintance; a good, strong type without subtlety or cynicism. During the early days inevitably a blunderer, his unselfish determination and transparent honesty secure a triumph in the end, for which Mr Walpole commands our complete sympathy. Robin's final capitulation indeed is ingeniously contrived to reveal excellent stuff in the boy—unsuspected beneath the imposed veneer.

It is a vigorous and attractive story, but Mr Walpole's variation upon a similar theme (in " The Green Mirror ") is, on the whole, more original, and—most emphatically, more modern. To begin with, Philip Mark lacks " obstinate courage," which is the backbone of a romance hero: he has, at bottom, no self-confidence. Like Harry, indeed, he boldly attacks the family citadel, and he too wants everybody to like him; but the ultimate victory is not his alone. The Trenchard defences, moreover, evince far greater diplomacy, although more vulnerable, being a House divided against itself. Not only does Philip love Katherine Trenchard, but she loves him, and even her foolish brother admires the man. The plot, in fact, develops into a duel, the more passionate for its perfect courtesy, between the travelled man of the world (who is yet a dreamer and an idealist) and the strangely gentle but overmastering personality of Mrs Trenchard, " who had been perfectly, admirably happy for fifty-six years." But she had been happy as a tyrant, and even when defeated could see " only her own determined invincibility."

From the first moment she had known Philip

as her enemy, the very figure whose appearance all her life she had dreaded; because he came from outside her sphere of influences. Too clever for frank hostility, which stiffens manhood, she concentrated her indomitable will upon annihilating his character, drawing him slowly but surely into the family net, moulding him after the approved pattern, stealing and breaking one by one every thought, vision, or feeling that was individually his own. She said, "Be one of us and you may have Katherine," affecting complete acceptance that she might utterly destroy.

And he, because he loved all the world, asking all the world to love him, because above all he loved the love of Katherine for this most wonderful mother of hers, would have accepted her terms—to his own undoing and Katherine's. Only the woman had greater courage and clearer vision. Victory was hard indeed—for it meant recognition of the crack in her knight's armour, the flaw in his manhood. She must herself do for them both—what he should have done for her; she must architect her own ideal. Wherefore, even while realising the utter finality of her decision, Katherine tells her lover "we've got to go, and now; we must escape or it will be too late." And they went—for ever.

Then Mrs Trenchard knew quite clearly that her ruling passion during all these months had not been, as she had supposed, her love of Katherine, but her hatred of Philip. She was beaten—beaten by her daughter, by a new generation, by a new age, beaten in the very moment of her victory.

Herein the cruelty of a great love.

Mr Walpole himself couples " The Green Mirror " with " The Duchess of Wrexe," as two records of an old family in conflict with the Spirit of Youth. " The Beaminsters (led by the Duchess) had been broken all in a moment because they had tried to do something that their age no longer permitted them to do. The Trenchards were much more difficult to break because they were not trying to do anything at all." All they wanted was to be—themselves. " I hate the new generation," says her ladyship; " the manly woman and the soft man with all this sentimental nonsense about caring for the people. Think of yourself, fight for yourself, keep up your pride—that's the only way the world's ever been run." It was the Beaminster ambition to run the world. "My grandmother," as Rachel remarked, " would have about three clever people, and then muddle all the rest, so that the three clever ones can have everything in their hands."

Her rôle is that of mysterious power in the background, a hidden hand; and critics of our author have found it difficult at times to accept the story of her domination. Hers was the tyranny of the best people, imposed without scruple upon the politics of her generation; a cynical old woman who liked hurting people.

But, indeed, the story is not in the main concerned with public affairs. It reveals revolt from within: the Duchess is beaten by her own family. Rachel, indeed, is from the beginning resentful, although horribly afraid. She never really admired, and always disliked, the old lady.

Trouble begins with her sympathy for Cousin Christopher, the black sheep of the family: lately returned in poverty from banishment. He is essentially a weak creature, boasting of his defiance and humbly eager to regain favour. Utterly without self-confidence, he poses as rebel, but would obviously accept terms. His expectation and his hope is for reconciliation, reinstatement. Rachel is warm-hearted and cousinly, it is her dream to make peace, and, mistaking an affectionate sense of justice for warmer feelings, Christopher loves and idealises the young girl.

The Duchess naturally has her suspicions, and seeks for her granddaughter's safety in marriage with Roddy Seddon, a rather simple-minded average young man, trained in the Beaminster traditions, and specially attached to the old lady. For himself, he must marry, " because Seddon Court must have a mistress, because he himself must have children, because he would like to have someone to be kind to." " What do you really care about? " asks Rachel, and he replies, " Oh, animals, and bein' out in the open, and shootin', and ridin', and fishin', or any old exercise—and comin' up to town for a buck every now and again; and then goin' back and seein' no one, and my old place, and—oh, I don't know."

"He had discovered when he was very young that nothing lasted, and that the things that lasted the shortest time were generally the best things," although with Rachel he claims a difference. "It doesn't matter really so much what I do, if I still like you best. Moments don't count, it's what goes on all the time that matters. Why, I might kiss a hundred women who matter nothing to me. I've never cared for anyone so long before," he added simply. And because she supposes that after all everybody's just the same, because she believes herself at heart a Beaminster, Rachel accepts the one way which seems open to her of escape from the haunting presence of the terrible old Duchess. As Lady Seddon, indeed, she finds that it takes a lot of years before married people settle down. Complications arise again with the "black sheep," still accepted as pet protégé, and it is not till Roddy is nearly killed on the hunting field that she learns to love and be happy. As a permanent invalid, the man develops strange sympathies and strength of character. He tackles the misunderstanding between them with big courage, plans a coup to confront the Duchess with Christopher, and earns the complete devotion of his high-spirited wife. Once more youth triumphs through the power of personality, and the old order is dead.

Whether intentionally or not Mr Walpole appears to produce his work in groups, and personally, at any rate, I cannot dissociate the two novels based on the somewhat melodramatic foundation of murder. Here, again, the catastrophe is brought about from motives directly in opposition to one another. Mr Perrin " thought he would surprise God by killing Traill, God would not be expecting that." He is, in fact, hopelessly morbid, if not insane. Years of monotonous existence in a miserably conducted private school, personal unpopularity, loneliness, and comparative failure, have bred in this worn out bundle of nerves a furious jealousy of youth, success, and good looks—all embodied in the new master. Traill easily secures the devotion of his pet pupils, without effort obtains the love of a girl whom the older man inarticulately worships, and quite unconsciously drives him to desperation. In the event both men are drowned and we have escaped no detail of horror. It is the most remorseless picture ever written of the deadening influences of absorption in school life.

" The Prelude to Adventure " reveals youth at its noblest (clean, wholesome, vigorous, almost normal) suddenly mastered by horror and disgust at the unclean beastliness in a hated school-fellow, carrying his trail of filth into undergraduate life.

The law, one imagines, would call this manslaughter: it was entirely without premeditation—the act of a moment. Olva Dune, nevertheless, did not doubt that he would be caught and delivered up to be hanged. When the miracle happens, and he entirely escapes suspicion, the memory of his deed simply destroys the man. He " carried his day through with a rush and a whirl so that he might be in bed almost before he had finished his dressing in the morning; no pause, no opportunity for silence." That is the atmosphere of the whole violent, restless story, a record of puzzled despair. The world certainly was well rid of his victim, but that brings no consolation. It is only, indeed, after he has fallen in love, confessed to his lady and been forgiven, learnt, too, that her mother has also killed an impossible husband (an inartistic coincidence) that Olva achieves hope. " Because I have broken the law I am an outlaw—out of touch with human society, until I have done something for human society. God has been telling me for many days that I owe a debt . . . God will show me . . . I must work out His order and then I will come back."

" Someone promised her " he would come back. Verily, to youth " all things are possible "; to age none.

If " Maradick at Forty " may seem to contradict this conclusion, its inconsistency is more apparent than actual. In some measure, certainly, the middle-aged hero renews his youth, and even permanently acquires a new personality. " You cannot imagine," the wife writes, " how improved dear old Jim is, really quite another man, and so amusing when he likes."

Yet Maradick has returned to the old grove. Under the mystic influence of Treliss (in Cornwall) he had experimented, on his own account, in youthfulness, only escaping disaster by a hair's-breadth. It was as the friend of youth itself, aiding romance and adventure, that he achieved heroism, and incidentally charm. He went far, did a big thing, but the harvest was not for him.

As Mr Walpole himself tells us (in three short passages entitled " Maradick "—*Daily News*, January, 1921) " for ten years "—after the Cornwall holiday—" he had been somnolent." He reappears as " the unhappy devil, your Philistine who would be the other thing . . . a perfectly neutral individual, scarcely a human being at all. People liked him, but always forgot him when he was not there, and he was considered a bore at dinner parties because he was so silent." In fact he led " an exceedingly lonely life."

Yet the fire in the man was not dead. He had been drugged, not murdered, by the " little woman," his wife, " who had lost her private character in her attempt to maintain a public appearance," and by the daughters he never had stopped to consider.

Once more the touch is given, the spark applied. He awakes to his daughter Vera. Blundering, at first, like the poor creature— average man—he yet perseveres, loving, wondering, and humbly tender, until " the most wonderful moment of his life occurred." Tightly the girl clasps his hand—" Oh, the times we're going to have, you and I. . . . The time we've wasted."

There Mr Walpole leaves him—once more born again. If not the full crop, there is at least grain for the grown man; a comforting, if a thin, harvest of adventure, shared with the heart of youth.

Mr Walpole, indeed, carries his faith in the dawn of life unto its very beginning. The whole story of " Jeremy " reveals no more than growth from cradle to the preparatory school. The child runs away from home with his naughty uncle, plagues his nurse, dominates over his sister, finds the grown-ups both stupid and puzzling. Here is keen sympathy, loving observation, light humour, and, curiously enough, quite sufficient material to fill over three hundred pages. The achievement, indeed, is the more remarkable because Jeremy is not unique, abnormal, or precocious, only quite human.

" The Golden Scarecrow," is more ambitious and less successful. The volume contains ten vignettes, all based upon one theme—" the friend about us in our infancy," the visitor from spheres before birth; whom for the few first years of life here below, some at least of us love and talk with till, as gradually we put away childish things growing in worldly wisdom, we too forget and deny. I am not sure whether the tender fancy will bear expression in prose narrative. Mr Walpole, at any rate, repeats himself and misses conviction.

There was, again, something of Russia in " The Green Mirror " : " it grows upon you, holds you, and at last begs you to stand up for it whenever it may be attacked "—he " found in Russia that the only thing demanded of him was that he should love his brother "—Russians " would talk for weeks." The woman Philip had known in Russia haunts, and for a time dominates, the whole atmosphere of his English life.

Wherefore he wrote " The Secret City," a magic tale of muddle and murder, tortured love, ideal patriotism, and unpractical self-sacrifice. Masterly pictures, concrete images. " Life is a tragedy to every Russian simply because the daily round is forgotten by him in his pursuit of an ultimate meaning." Marovitch thanks God he has no " sense of decency, and no Russian has any sense of decency, and that is why we are beaten and despised by the whole world, and yet are finer than them all." The woman, unhappily married, cries out : " I love him so that I am blind for him, and deaf for him, and dead for him. Before it is too late I want it—I want him—I want happiness." It may be Russia has drawn Mr Walpole, just through the eager adventuring of her children after the unattainable. English Clare's no less imperious demand for happiness, on the other hand, means being always afraid, puts her for ever among the stay-at-homes. " Fortitude " shows her a drag, clinging to Peter, jealous though proud of his work, hating the friends of his childhood.

It is clearly inevitable that any picture of genius should be concerned with the struggle between Art and Life! The choice whether a man shall express himself and comparatively neglect wife and family; or sacrifice at least something of his revelation to personal ties. This is, indeed, almost a side issue here (though treated with passionate intensity) since Peter was haunted from birth by the diabolical cruelty of a horrible old father, sitting at home "willing disaster," cursed "by the instincts of a rotten family, three parts of us aching to go to the bad." Adventure for him means a tempest, shouting and fighting after the Finest Thing, nothing of happiness or satisfaction. Always he must be "The Rider on the Lion."

Until out of the heart of the storm there came voices, "Blessed be Pain and Torment—Plague and Pestilence—Loss and Failure, all Sorrows, Torments, Hardships, Endurances that demand Courage. Blessed be these things, for of these things cometh the breaking of a man."

There is in Peter something of Tom Jones and Peregrine Pickle. He is a knight-errant, a Don Quixote, the explorer travelling ever with his life in his hands, knocking always at the gates of Heaven.

Cornwall, moreover, nearly breaks him, though it spiritualised Maradick; poverty and want strike at him, men and women scourge him.

Fed on books in childhood, he one day casts them behind him, plunging into a whirlpool of surmise about himself. Later he caught the disease of the Terror of London. For him the most splendid things in the world are the most terrible. Wherefore, alone, he is tremendous, victorious.

In his thumb-nail " Portraits of the Period " Mr Walpole attempts what one may call an impressionist study of life " after the war." There are characters in these grim tales we know from earlier volumes; one, indeed, being entirely concerned with Peter Westcott of " Fortitude," but plainly they are not meant to picture any complete new world. Only a chance phrase, here and there, reveals a halting hope of some general, and quite vaguely realised, advance.

Peter, indeed, hating the " tawdry fustian sentimentality " of men who succeed like Edmund Robsart, finding himself shelved by the querulous, heavy-eyed new school, reads a message in the bright noise of London. To him, it seemed " all men were children, playing with toys—toy policemen and toy omnibuses. Life was a nursery. Perhaps there would be a new world—somewhere, someday. Meanwhile there was enough to do, keeping the nursery in order, seeing the weak babies were not trodden upon, making sure no one cried himself to sleep." He would not expect the millennium.

The Hon. Clive Torby fondly imagined it was " about time that some of us enjoyed ourselves, after what we've been through," and went mad about dancing. But, being at bottom a thoroughly good sort, took to house-painting and, with real heroism, refused to live on a fond mother. " Lois Drake," who had pictured a new world full of male women, found the " old-fashioned nonsense " was *not* all over, and had to yield her lover to the most feminine of friends. Fanny Close, portress, gave up the " job " she loved to the " demobbed," and " secured one from which no man in the world would have the right to oust her."

Only the old, who have done and been nothing all their lives, can find no place after the war. Absolom Jay declared that " Britain *couldn't be beaten*, which meant that he must be assured of his comforts. . . . He hated the lower classes . . . the very sight of a working man threw him into a frenzy." Yet the Society for which he lived would have none of him. " They would chloroform everyone over sixty. They'd had enough of the old duds messing all the world up. . . . He gave them the creeps." And " young " people " looked right through him, as though he were an uneasy and disturbing ghost.'" So he crept home in a tube, was jostled beyond bearing, lay on his sofa and died.

And Miss Morganhurst, bridge-player and scandalmonger. Furiously, she ignored the war, would not speak of it; and such grim repression turned her brain. The " wild beasts leapt on her imagination. . . . Every horror, every indecency, every violation of truth and horror, seemed to have lodged in that brain. Every murder, every rape, every slaughter of innocent children, every violation of girls and old women—they were all there. . . . *I was there* you know," she whispered to the doctor. And she died next day.

" After the war," it seems only reality can

live. Shadows of men and women, the drones of life, those who have preyed, in idleness, upon others, are now called to their account.

We must not, however, omit Mrs Porter and Miss Allen, which—though somewhat apart from these tales, is perhaps more powerful than any. Suddenly left a desolate (but wealthy) war widow, absolutely without happy memories, the dearest of old ladies bravely determines to live " right in the very middle of things." Selecting the perfect companion, Miss Allen, she will throw in her lot with the young, and rejoice in their joy. Only it may not be. The late Mr Porter had been " the complete brute "; he brought his mistresses to the house, and taunted his wife with looking down on him. Knowing a weak heart might carry him off at any moment, he said I will leave you all my money, and then " just as you begin to enjoy it I will come and fetch you." Always the poor woman was tortured with dread. She knew he would—and he did. Only so long as Miss Allen was brave and strong enough to *pretend* she saw nothing, her loyal devotion kept the trembling widow alive. But it broke her nerve, she failed at last to deceive her old friend—and so lost her. It is an eerie record that grips one. The fiendish malignity of the silent ghost, his quiet and certainty, overwhelm the imagination. Mr Walpole compels belief, and confounds the sceptic. Because he makes no comment.

I am disposed to think that in " The Captives " Mr Walpole has attempted something bigger than ever before, and, in a large measure, he achieves success. There is, here, a very clearly defined purpose, carried out with grim thoroughness. He has created an atmosphere that will live. The intense cruelty, selfishness, and egotism of some religious people is not, of course, a new subject; but Mr Walpole has been unusually successful in catching the spiritual behind the formalism. There is colour and warmth in his exposure of the cold, hard surface. Individually, the religious may, naturally, be either sincere or hypocritical, designing or superstitious. Mr Walpole presents all types: always without strain or exaggeration. The mysterious influence, moreover, is alive in material things. " It's in the house, it's in the rooms, it's in the very furniture."

Finally there is a *real* force somewhere. You may deny God, you may despise His worshippers; but there is *something* in it: something that holds you captive, torturing, tempting, possessing your very soul. They may be right after all. The hidden Power is there. To accentuate the all-pervading impression, Mr Walpole has placed his heroine, Maggie, in the centre of the picture; a being utterly untaught, uncivilised: a child of nature; pre-eminently susceptible yet with a vivid personality and iron will. As a child dependent upon an utterly immoral country clergyman, her father; knowing kindness and affection from none save a drunken uncle; she is suddenly transplanted into the home of a holy visionary, the stately, cold-mannered Aunt Anne,

Inner Saint of the Chapel, which accepted the Second Coming. Here, indeed, there is love, highly spiritualised, and some measure of tenderness. But you live in a cage, cut off absolutely from man and the world: a sense always that they are waiting to spring out on you, chain you down, swallow you up once and for all.

Now, hitherto, Maggie "had always made the best of everything, because she had never had an intimate friend to tell her that it was a foolish thing to do." Wherefore she tries, honestly, to love and be loved; strives, in small matters, to improve herself. Only the basis of her nature is independence: the determination to secure liberty, to be herself. So that for her, life means perpetual struggle.

There follows a new element of experience. Obviously such a character must find "the man," not to lean on, but mother. Here her instinct will be swift and sure, unreasoning, without calculation—" Her feeling for him was almost sexless. . . . She was so simple as to be shameless, and at once, if he had asked her then in the street to marry him, she would have said yes without hesitation, or fear, or any analysis." Henceforth, in fact, there remains no other motive or interest in life for her. " The whole thing is that I love you . . . I'd be poor enough if my love for you just depended on your being good to me and all the rest of it . . . it can't be arything that you can do that can alter it." There is no judgment or criticism here, no concern with his past (which, as it happens, had been weak and wild); no demand for heroism, or even fidelity, in the future. So long as he wants her, she is ready, and, as she believes, he will always want her. It does not frighten her that he is already married, because, as his wife has deserted him, there can be no robbery. Between themselves, all is well; since Martin, always hesitating and repentant in his relation to others, has no doubt of her.

Inevitably, religion is up in arms. Aunt Anne subtly exerts her influence; and though never distracted from her position, Maggie is trapped through her affections and her tenderness towards the suffering, into some dangerous delay. It is dangerous, not for herself, but for Martin, since he, too, knows the demon of Faith. Throughout his muddled existence, the man clung always to the love of his father, the saintly minister of Aunt Anne's Chapel, a seer and a prophet, starving himself for love of God. As a child, indeed, Martin had been paraded as a Pious Prodigy and, though reaction drove him to dissipation, the chain held. He knew, like Maggie, there was *something*.

When the old man dies suddenly, Martin is seized with the mad idea of responsibility for his death. Literally possessed by repentance, he passionately renounces even his love: since he hurt and injured all he cared for, *he would not allow himself to care for her*. In the horror of loneliness among the Saints, Maggie suffers a period of utter abandon; but soon rallying her forces, utters this strange, brave ultimatum:

HUGH WALPOLE

" I'm going to make my own life and have a good time—and never stop loving Martin for one single second."

She does *not* stop loving, but she has a thoroughly bad time. In my judgment, Mr Walpole at this point loses grip of the character. Trusting to the motherly instincts of his heroine, he tells how Maggie married a weak, good-natured, but rather unpleasant, middle-aged clergyman; naturally telling him she had no love to give, but idly thinking she could make him happy. Incidentally Paul ardently desires her love, but he has been always ruled by a domineering, foolish, and narrow-minded sister, who continues to live with them. Maggie, in fact, abandons at once any attempt to " make her own life," weakly seizes the first " occupation " (to play the mother) that offers, and proves false to her own instinct. I cannot admit this. The Maggie of these chapters is another person, similar but not the same. In fact this part should be read as a separate novel, such as George Eliot embedded in " Middlemarch," simply diverting the current of events. A little masterpiece (for on its own merits the episode is a fine piece of work), complete in itself, but out of place. Curiously enough, too, Mr Walpole brings into this episode Katherine Mark (formerly Trenchard), the heroine of " The Green Mirror," and defames her character. This kindly, managing, but self-absorbed Katherine is *not* the woman who dominated the earlier novel, where she revealed no hint of such a pitiful degeneration.

Mr Walpole, however, recovers himself in the end, resurrecting the real Maggie. When she learns that Martin has come to England, and can be traced, there is not a moment's hesitation. Regarding her own husband no more than she had feared her man's wife, she immediately takes her place at her lover's side. More than ever a wreck, moral and physical, the man at first will have none of her; and, indeed, by brusque moroseness nearly drives her finally out of his life. Only at last when, confessing herself beaten, Maggie prepares to take him at his own word, reserves give way. "I have fought," he cries, "but I can fight no longer. Stay, at your own risk! I must be selfish. I want you." For her then there was no hesitation, no more need be said. We leave her; clearly aware, indeed, of the difficulties, never supposing for one moment that he would suddenly become a reformed character; yet supreme in her content. She had found her place in the world, her work to do. It was enough.

Rejecting the episode-marriage, this is a great, original character, finely conceived, and drawn with remarkable power. There are firm, sure outlines: no strain or exaggeration. Perhaps even greater insight was needed to picture Martin's instability without losing our sympathy. He is, superficially, a poor creature: only she read through appearances and she was right. We are confident that, in the end, she made a man of him, worth the making. Her single purpose, her primitive instinct, balanced by naïve shrewdness of insight, made up a spiritual force that was no less invincible, than unerring in aim.

We cannot, as a whole, regard Mr Walpole as a typical modern novelist. He works with the old material, character studies from observation, not self-revealing. A composed plot, dramatic construction, a set subject, a defined purpose, almost a moral. He deals with facts, words, appearances, crises and the exceptional. He uses rapid movement, strong local colour or atmosphere, and does not despise melodrama. There is, of course, subtlety in abundance, continual soul analysis, and the Ideal of Self. Only these are symptoms of his age, not the web of his art. As a craftsman he accepts broadly the tradition of novel writing; following it with masterly skill : building thereon great work.

He accepts, too, much from Romance, which Realism holds in derision; gaining thereby an invigorating vitality which we do not find in some, at least, of his contemporaries.

Indeed, his latest book, "The Young Enchanted," might fairly be described as a sincere, and exceptionally delightful, romance almost throughout. Only the furniture of the narrative, its dialogue, events, and superficial local colour, are actually of to-day and carefully drawn from observation.

In one of his " Portraits of the Period " Mr Walpole revived Peter Westcott from " Fortitude " when he announced his determination to look after weak babies in the nursery of life.

He nobly redeems the promise in "The Young Enchanted." Here again we are shown the first youth of Henry and Millie Trenchard from "The Green Mirror"—two incurable romantics. The boy, indeed, is the most complete knight-errant ever conceived. For him, this is a strange tale of "the unselfish devotion of his passion for Christina. The first love is not the only love, but it is often the only love into which self does not enter." He had guarded her with patient gallantry from the moment her sad eyes roused his manhood; and when the time came, snatched her away from her wicked mother, stayed with her "in silence and without moving" until her big, kind uncle came and "took her home" to Denmark. He is Sir Galahad and Don Quixote in London to-day; but transparently sincere, vitally real, and not in the least absurd.

Millie's romance is almost commonplace in comparison, but her personality supplies the charm. Innocence led her to fall in love with a cheap and vulgar villain without a scrap of originality in his composition. She persists in loyalty, long after all her instincts have *felt* the truth; but dismisses him with stern decision the moment the facts emerge. We leave her "not happier exactly, but quiet again," imagining, for herself, that is "almost all she cares about now." But the awakening has not killed her power for joy—"Oh! life's wonderful! How anyone can be bored I can't think. The things that go on, and the people, and these wonderful times. Why, I'm only at the beginning—at the beginning of myself, at the beginning of the world, at the beginning of everything! What a time to be alive again."

It is Peter Westcott, a new Peter—born again to his youth and at work on another great novel—who, awakened by their affectionate vitality, guides these young innocents through the glare and bustle of daily life.

Mr Walpole suggests, indeed, that in the end Millie will find her happiness in returning his love; but many readers, we fear, will judge him too old for the part.

Here, as always elsewhere, Mr Walpole constructs a strong, original, and imaginative plot, that reveals the real life of real people, artistically dramatic. The central theme, too, is supported with all his usual wealth of interesting and vital minor " persons of the drama "; continuing, in one important group, his favourite theme of a fine " old family," who still stand to prove that " the past is not dead, that it must go on with its beauty and pathos, influencing, interpenetrating the present." Even the young cannot " begin the world again as though nothing had ever happened before."

THE WOODEN HORSE	1909
MARADICK AT FORTY	1910
MR PERRIN AND MR TRAILL	1911
THE PRELUDE TO ADVENTURE	1912
FORTITUDE	1913
THE DUCHESS OF WREXE	1914
THE GOLDEN SCARECROW	1915
THE DARK FOREST	1916

THE GREEN MIRROR	1918
THE SECRET CITY	1919
JEREMY	1919
MARADICK	1920
THE CAPTIVES	1921
PORTRAITS OF THE PERIOD	1921
THE YOUNG ENCHANTED	1921

W. L. GEORGE

THERE is a difficulty in appreciating Mr W. L. George, because he is always tempting one to argue with him. His own volumes of criticism, moreover, reveal that he holds precise *theories* on fiction; for, as he puts it, " ashamed as we are of the novel with a purpose, we can no longer write novels without a purpose."

He finds " more that is honest and helpful in a single page of ' Tono Bungay ' than in all the great Victorians put together "; while, on a first reading of this novel, one of his heroines experienced " a fierce, concentrated joy, as if in a nightmare she had been stifling under the blankets and somebody had suddenly come, pulled away the hateful hot weight, and she had seen, high above, the star-studded sky."

Now Mr George is always very determined to " lift the blankets "; but he does *not* carry us into the open air. His idea of life is " just one damn thing after another," and " most vivid when most unpleasant," which is precisely the view of his own " realists who have won fame by seeing the dunghill very well, and not at all the spreading chestnut tree above."

Curiously enough, as it seems to me, the men novelists are, nearly all of them, still entangled within the " problem "—as we discovered it when playwrights first turned preachers. They want " as many scenes in the bedroom as in the drawing-room," and complete freedom to discuss the " main pre-occupation of life "—which is " sex." At present, they urge, " conversation is over-sexed, the novel is under-sexed, therefore untrue, therefore insincere "—the familiar cry of a past decade.

Now Mr George maintains that " we novelists are the showmen of life "; he proclaims Miss Sheila Kaye-Smith " the true novelist, the showman of life "; he declares that " the novel does day by day express mankind, and mankind in the making . . . always it is the showman of life "—all of which obviously recalls Thackeray. Yet the younger men attempt, not always successfully, " to crush within the covers of an octavo volume the whole of the globe spinning round its axis, to express with an attitude the philosophy of life, to preach by gospel rather than by statement."

That is to say, we are realists to-day; not in the service of art, but as missionaries and prophets. The novelist must search after, and express, the whole truth, and he must *use* truth for edification.

There can be no question that Mr George has many convictions. Primarily he is a good hater —in the spirit of democracy. " The Second Blooming," for example, contains—and, indeed, largely depends on—an almost savage picture of the useless activities, the idle busyness, by which Society women are moved to drug discontent. " A Bed of Roses " and " The Confessions of Ursula Trent " reveal the brutality with which civilisation would crush independence in women, and the cynical, cold-blooded revenge open to them. " A Blind Alley " illustrates class-war as developed in special phases during the war, and " A Stranger's Wedding " touches a failure to bridge the gulf.

In fact, " class " and " sex " are the main props of Mr George's armoury: sex largely predominating. He is eloquent, indeed, concerning the idle rich:

> " There were many of these beautiful, well-gowned, detached women who seem a typical product of English civilisation. Carefully they preside over social functions; they assist at political meetings. . . . They read, without partisanship, the book of the day; they go to picture shows and buy pictures when the artist is an acquaintance; they love their daughters, send them to the right schools, marry them to the right men; they love their sons and direct their tastes towards the right regiments. Strictly, they are organisers of the governing classes, they are the people who take orders from men and make them a little more human; they form against the threatening desire for reform which the working-class growls out now and then in the shape of an incoherent, impotent strike, a broad bulwark of refinement which is strong by the very fact of its lukewarm, of its rather faded, eloquence. It is almost as if these ladies stood in front of the dockers, clamouring for an extra penny, raised a deprecatory finger, and said, ' Hush! What naughty words! '

F

> And so gracefully do they stand, so assured that their class will always stand, that, after a few growls, the docker goes, very much like the lion that noses its prey and, finding that it seems to be dead, leaves it alone. It is enough to wonder whether these ladies, and all those whom they represent, are not indeed corpses, shamming life with amazing skill."

In the story from which these bitter phrases are taken, Mr George, indeed, is mainly concerned in revealing the failure of such " busyness " to satisfy the " beautiful " women. But the scorn for Society implied therein is strong and sincere. The heroine of " The Stranger's Wedding " proves exceptional understanding of real purity and refinement in " common " people, as " A Bed of Roses " exposes the real curse of poverty.

Mr George, in fact, is a genuine democrat; and if his condemnation of wealth and convention is too sweeping, if he ignores the ideal behind progress, his anger is righteous, the evil he would smite does exist. In the problems of class-warfare, his sympathies are sound, his condemnation is just.

Concerning sex, however, he is less balanced, more given to cant :

> " Love is outside marriage," cries Fenor, " because love's too big to stay inside . . . don't you see that of itself it carries the one sanctity that may exist between men and women? That it cannot be bound because it is as light as air, imponderable, so fierce that all things it touches it burns, so sweet that whosoever hath drunk shall ever more be thirsty? "

That is the false premis on which all pleas for licence and incontinence are established : the red flag of perverse realism. We do *not* see, and we do not believe.

Woman suffers, thinks Mr George, because she cannot

> " understand love in its neurotic moods; she cannot yet understand that a greater intensity might creep into passion if one *knew it to be transient,* that one might love more urgently, with greater fierceness, if one knew that soon the body, temple of that love, would fade, wither, die, then decay . . . that haste to live made living more intense."

Man, on the other hand, accepts the fact that the same woman can " no longer give him adventure." He sees, what he had always known must happen, that " they had lapsed into a relation which slowly from irregular grew regular. It was not marriage, but it was in the nature of marriage." Now, " after two and a half years . . . she had done wifely things for him. . . . Love and domestic economy : it was very like marriage after all."

And, *therefore*, he will have no more of it. Obviously, we can deduct arguments for, or against, marriage from this basis. Mr George adopts the latter course.

> " You see, when you marry a man you give him a glorious wedding-garment; his new morning-coat and the orchid in his buttonhole, they aren't in it by the side of that garment, and he can't go round to some heavenly tailor and order another. It just gets older and dustier and more bedraggled, and he can't even take it off; you've got to see him in

his old wedding-garment, all stained with tears and blood, stained where the acid of angry words has fallen, and crumpled in the places which ought to have been unfolded now and then, but haven't been touched for years. You can't forgive that, you know, you can't forgive marriage because the early rapture has gone out of it, nor Eros who used to sweep above your head, deafening you with the beating of his wings; you can't forgive him when he begins to moult. You never believe that his feathers will grow again, and you're right, for they don't."

In the end they become "*busy with other things, these two, and husband and wife only by the way.*"

After all, such a false view of life follows logically from the conviction that " men have no use for women save as mistresses," only recognising love as a sex-conflict, a wild passion wherein he " had to make war, to conquer." Here, too, the woman begs him " to hurt her, to set his imprint upon her "; wanting " a real man." He may lift his elbow a bit and all that, but anyhow he's a man. It is just for this reason, indeed, that in Beowulf Buildings they prefer marriage : " If yer lives alone nothing 'appens . . . stuck in the mud like. But when yer've got a 'usband, things 'as wot they calls a zest . . . if 'e do come 'ome . . . p'r'aps 'e'll give yer one in the mouf. Variety, that's wot it is, mum, variety . . . there ain't no life where there ain't no variety." Even the woman " about to conquer " must wear " the slave look."

Man expects " marriage to be the great

solution, to be wafted by the Registrar's wand into a world where everything—games, society, household, art, sick-nursing, travel-bureau—will be available for you when you press a button. Or, better still, where everything works so smoothly that you have only to tell your wife to press the button. It's not a woman a man ought to marry, it's William Whiteley's." Because he begins by being " just sensuous, feeling and hearing, smelling, seeing, an animal with the intellectual faculties of man added to heighten the animal's enjoyment," their " nominally sexless and deeply sensual associations . . . always on the edge of mutual conquest," were " always robbed of mystery and delight when long-balked attraction came to a tardy blooming."

The manner varies, but everywhere Mr George sees men, women, and life as he has painted them in his terrible " Bed of Roses."

" Men," says Victoria, may " have us as breeders and housekeepers, but the mistress is the root of all." She can recognise every variety of " the merely brutal glance by which a man takes stock of a woman's charms." In luxury she " feels smooth, *stroked*, lazily voluptuous; a finer animal, more beautiful as men understand beauty."

Her " touch soft as velvet, her grip hard as steel," she will exploit mankind, spare none, offer no quarter, give them a taste of the whip : " A woman commands nothing but what she can get out of man's senses."

It is always—more delicately expressed—

"woman tainting man, making him strut, just as he, in return, made her look through her eyelashes."

For all its sincerity, despite the justice of woman's revenge, one can scarcely avoid feeling that, after all, Victoria brought things upon herself. Strictly speaking, she was not actually driven into the paths she trod. The same criticism may be applied, with far greater emphasis, to the " Confessions of Ursula Trent," who simply ran away from a happy, if boring, home. She is described, moreover, as a cultured and clever woman, with all the instincts of the County; and we are told, again and again, that she was " no good " with men, she had " no courage," was only " a damned lady." Whereas, in fact, she reveals absolutely no restraint or refinement from beginning to end. " I can't sell myself," she cries with scorn, but does nothing else. Stretching " out her hands for love, she found lovers," and very soon came " to think that there's no such thing as a pure-minded girl." Marriage is " only a dodge for getting rid of being in love," which itself means " waking up in the middle of the night and running about the room like a crazy thing because I've dreamed he's with some other girl . . . feeling all soft and swoony just because he's helped you into the bus by the elbow." In fact, " most marriages are merely evidence that the girl has held out." What she calls her " class cowardice " only hampered her with married men : " If he had been a bachelor I could have given way to him," as to others. There is no reason whatever why, at one moment, she "had an idea that there wouldn't be quite enough room in the car for Sir Charles, myself, and my self-respect," when, at others, she "just didn't care."

There is absolutely no backbone or character in Miss Ursula Trent. She was simply out for joy all the time, and excused herself by declaring that "a woman can scratch up a living but not a future, and the only job she's really fit for is to be a man's keep, legal or illegal, permanent or temporary."

We have, in fact, nearly three hundred pages about her many "temporaries" and scarcely a dozen for the one permanent. Ursula, herself, declares with passion that, though "men all want the same thing," Alec is really different: "Indeed, he is my lover . . . but he is to me a man as well as a lover. He is my companion and my dear. I wish I could tell him how dear he is to me, my workaday lover, my comrade, my future, and my reality." To him she was "the only woman in the world that I could love if she was old, if she was ugly, if she was lying, if she was faithless. See what I mean?"

For my part, I cannot believe he will "last so long" as the handsome and faithless Julian of earlier days. Mr George, at least, makes absolutely no attempt to distinguish their emotions; and Ursula's protestations only confirm one's doubt. She was attracted, loosely and sensually, precisely as by the others. He was, in a way, a change.

If that is all the modern novelist can find in Love, they had far better confine themselves to passion-pictures. The *pretence* here spoils the book.

It would not, indeed, be fair to say that Mr George exults in mere physical passion. Few writers, indeed, have exposed it with so much force. Yet it haunts his imagination, almost to the exclusion of all else. For his own work, as in criticising others, he follows the older realists in a most morbid and perverse exaggeration of the part it plays in the ordinary life of ordinary people. He will not recognise the ideal of marriage which is love grown deeper, not more perfunctory, by closer intimacy, larger experience, greater knowledge; passion intensified, not killed, by fruition. He sees, always and everywhere, sex-conflict which must conquer and take : missing the union of sex, which is the heart of love; always giving, seeking, and finding more to give.

Knowing that conquest can never satisfy, he yet will not admit the power of sacrifice and restraint; the true happiness born of more intimate understanding, more complete trust : of two who become one. Not creatures of habit are these; not content because indifferent, not satisfied because sluggish; but since they remain young, always giving each other adventure.

The realists, of course, were right in rejecting the " covered " romance and false sentiment of

Victorian respectability; right, above all, in facing and stating the power of passion upon men and women alike. But they defined passion as something separate and distinct from that love of which it is, in fact, only a part: thereby limiting, and degrading, both. Not unnaturally, perhaps, they exaggerated the importance of their own discovery; extracting new insincerities out of a new truth; new cant and convention from the ruins of the old.

Mr George, indeed, almost appears to regard the ordinary concerns of life (even including marriage and children) as a tiresome and degrading interruption to the pursuit for which he conceives us best fitted—sex-experience; which means conflict, conquest, and satiety. He nowhere attempts to picture a "happy" marriage, or any permanent love. Only the three husbands in "Second Blooming," and the hero of "Blind Alley," take any interest in affairs, while their material success is commonplace. Their ambitions are absolutely self-centred. Sir Henry thoroughly disliked, and distrusted, anything *extra*-ordinary: "all roads in Edward's mind led back to Edward": the rest are nonentities. For such the importance of passion appears plausible: they have no other outlet, and provide none—for their wives or their daughters.

It is not suggested, on the other hand, that Mr George's characters are any way lacking in personality. They are very convincingly human, and he can tell an excellent tale: far more briskly and dramatically than most contemporary novelists. The books all reveal, incidentally, strong political bias; but are, otherwise, purely emotional. There are, here, no great men, no little problems and, practically, no home life.

Twice, indeed, Mr George varies his atmosphere by interesting studies of French character. " A City of Light," laid in Paris, throws most fascinating side-lights upon *the* problem, by its careful analysis of the marriage-theory among the French. The hero and heroine, far more " knowing " than would be their English brothers and sisters of the same age and circumstances, are yet almost phenomenally simple and good at heart. For them, apparently, marriage means happiness, chiefly because they were always calm. M. Cardoresse, on the other hand, in " The Making of an Englishman," is so far carried away by his enthusiasm for John Bull as to openly glory in the wife of his choice. His native attitude towards other women, indeed, is indulged freely (offering fine occasion for satire upon British conventions), but his inconstancy is pre-nuptial. England—and Ethel—remain ideal. The story throughout is very humorous, and most subtle.

In " Caliban " Mr George retains all that peculiar, almost brutal, forcefulness which characterises most of his work. He stands almost alone, I think, among his contemporaries in the passionate sincerity of his convictions. They are, indeed, like those of his latest hero, chiefly expressed by the determination to " smash up " something—" traditions that just lie about and block the road." But on the other hand, all he hates deserves hatred, and so much fury over waste implies belief in the higher possibilities of human nature.

This is the riotous story of a man made drunk by his own success and then intoxicated by the war. In the precise words of the hero in an earlier novel he finds life " one damned exciting thing after another."

Richard Bulmer belongs to a type common in fiction : the man who smashes the world single-handed. But the variety is up-to-date : being the Press Incarnate, a colossal Publicity Man, maker of a thousand newspapers that all hit the bull's eye. He is intensely commonplace, but supernaturally smart; so that he easily leads a long-suffering public by the nose. Only one thing distinguishes him from every man; he knows what he wants, and how to get it. What he gets he gives—with zip, filling his own pockets in the process : though, indeed, he cares little or nothing about the money itself, save as an instrument of power—the power to shout and smash.

One can forgive the man's innate vulgarity, for the keen boyish enjoyment of his restless audacity. Every paper he projects, every startling idea he gets hold of, is like a new toy to him; and the zest of the game never wavers. Somewhere back of his mind, too, lurks a vision of Utopia. There is in him no shred of imagination, no sense of beauty; but he is a genuine democrat. In his own blustering, domineering fashion he loves the great B.P., while he despises them—" one's got to mislead people if one wants to lead them . . . I'm for democracy I am."

He would rebuild England—" no small farms and small holdings, but great grain farms with cornfields twenty miles long and electric ploughs to make the furrows . . . a model bathroom, electric light, etc. Uniform if possible, the labourers to be privates and the foremen sergeants and the managers to have commissions. . . . Send your letter by aeroplane. And lay out your town properly. Cut all the streets at right angles, and call them by their numbers. Have a store every five hundred yards exactly, and a public house every half-mile. Order, we want order. We want the shop at the corner to be the tailor, the next the butcher, the next the grocer, the next the barber, and so on. All over the town, all over the country, all over the world. Same language in London and Abyssinia. Same sort of shirt along the same latitude. Food to be regulated according to temperature—and no more of those fanciful local variations."

Then things began to happen, enormously exciting things, and Mr George diverts his energies to a vehement assault on politics and the war, with his accustomed impatience; and, simply ignoring movement beneath the surface, or emotions that have not as yet found voice, he noisily " damns " a world that had " fallen into the claws of brutal cynicism, snaky finesse, and filthy gold-dust, with the three B's that make

Empire—beer, bible, bayonet—joined in symbolic panoply."

Bulmer was "happy in these days." His papers became hysterical, daily turning a somersault. He would proclaim " The Man," who in a few weeks became ignoble. . . . The man became " The Worm," then he sought another man. " While his friend the Premier's " political style " was more akin to skirt dancing."

" Still there was between the two men a kinship of temperament : both were capricious, both unable to keep their hands off other men's jobs ; both were convinced that they alone could give a policy its finishing touch. Bulmer was given to smashing things, and Eastcombe to ignoring them, but in any case the things toppled."

The portraiture here is obvious enough though Mr George—inartistically—presents Bulmer as Lord Northcliffe's rival, jealous of his successes ; and introduces Mr Lloyd George by name.

Throughout the whole novel, indeed, we see the hero as a public man ; we are concerned with his work in the world, his outward seeming, his surface character ; yet he, too, does not entirely escape the eternal sex-problem. Bulmer, indeed, has not much use for women ; because they are secret, and " if a thing was secret it was antipathetic to publicity."

Nevertheless he marries the " upholstress with her sullen, sensuous beauty " ; because she was always ready to smile and listen when he talked about his ambitions, before anyone else believed in him : and they are admirably suited—up to a point. She enjoys spending money, and satisfies his unexacting demands on the sex. After a time, however, she realises how little she means to him, and as they drift into a separation, he for his part discovers an ideal woman in the cultured, young, and beautiful widow who was born to Society and Social Influence. Mr George devotes considerable care to the analysis of Eleanor.

Like all women of broad sympathies and quick courage, she is intrigued by the man's ruthless power, his frank self-absorption and boyish indifference to the rest of the world; while every instinct of her inherited and acquired taste shrinks from the coarse fibre of his nature. The issue remains in doubt almost to the last chapter, and it is certainly hinted that had not his intense excitement over the " jolly war " thrown him a little off his balance, she might have risked the experiment. As things are she concludes that, after all, she could never be more than a triumphant episode in his career—" the memory of a night—like his wife," and the position is not attractive.

Wherefore she leaves him—furious but not despairing, baffled but not beaten : ready for more adventure and new spheres to annex : " One doesn't hitch on to anybody, one just messes about a bit in the middle of life, and life sails away."

It is the Epitaph of the Egoist.

Mr George, perhaps, would be a greater artist if the preacher in him were less obtrusive. But his work is virile, original, and quite sincere.

W. L. GEORGE

He is not, I think, anywhere false to humanity: only his sense of proportion has gone astray. His characters are quite real, quite true; but they are rather (at different extremes) exceptional than average, strained than normal. They certainly do not represent life or humanity as a whole; nor even a generation complete. For the dramatic purpose they are, indeed, varied sufficiently. Each novel is interesting in itself; quite independent of any other: only the variation remains circular.

Finally, I cannot resist quoting against himself Mr George's most just criticism of D. H. Lawrence: "He is clamouring within the narrow limits of his incident . . . it is true, but it is not general . . . because a thing is, he believes that it is; when a thing is, it may only be accidental; it may be particular. . . . The novelist should select among the particular that which has application to the general. . . . Amazing charge to make against a novelist that his persons are too much persons! But persons must partly be types, or else they become monsters!"

A BED OF ROSES	1911
THE CITY OF LIGHT	1912
ISRAEL KALISCH	1913
THE MAKING OF AN ENGLISHMAN	1914
THE SECOND BLOOMING	1914
OLGA NAZIMOV	1915
THE STRANGER'S WEDDING	1916
BLIND ALLEY	1919
CALIBAN	1920
THE CONFESSIONS OF URSULA TRENT	1921

J. D. BERESFORD

THERE is always an obvious danger in labels; though the temptation to grouping, since one must compare, becomes at times well-nigh irresistible. Mr W. L. George has divided modern novelists into " self-exploiters, mirror-bearers, and commentators " : of whom those with most promise " stand midway between the expression of life and the expression of themselves; indeed, they try to express both, to achieve art by criticising life; they attempt to take nature into partnership."

Mr Beresford, certainly, is both a conventional novelist—in the accepted sense of the story-teller—and a modern analytic : at once reflecting and critical. He works through both mediums—self-expression and imagination or, more strictly, invention. He is, both ways, somewhat laboured, after the manner of his day, but he does not neglect either dramatic effects or firm characterisation.

Jacob Stahl, whom one assumes himself, is elaborately set out in *three* novels; and there is really no reason why he should not continue the subject indefinitely, after the manner of Miss Richardson : because " Jacob was ever at the beginning of life." He could never settle in a groove.

On the other hand, "God's Counterpoint" is a genuine creation. Philip, perhaps, is not *quite* human; but the conception has a very marked originality, is consistently maintained, and produces pure drama. It touches, moreover, upon the pre-occupation with sex in a spirit that is both independent and sincere.

In "Housemates" I fancy that we may recognise Stahl—under a new name; in circumstances which, if similar, are yet sufficiently diverse. It is not, in fact, the *same* man: but one with many of the same characteristics, offering very similar occasions for sympathy.

"The Hampdenshire Wonder" stands plainly apart, as mere fantasy. Here Mr Beresford plays with psychology as Wells and others have played with science: carrying invention beyond reality, whence to philosophise upon the abstract.

His later story, "The Jervaise Comedy," is frankly a trifle: wooing the spirit of comedy to expose pride. It is a clever enough piece of work, but might have been written by many, almost at any time.

"These Lynnekers" is no less pure observation than "God's Counterpoint"; but less concentrated and, in one sense, more ordinary. It is based, in fact, on that time-honoured framework of opposition between the hero and his family: they are all slaves to the herd instinct, he alone taking an independent, superior line of conduct. "The House in Demetrius Road," too, stands alone as a study in personality—ruined by drink, with the devotion accorded the " real " man.

Whatever his mood, however, Mr Beresford writes with assurance. He is not, I imagine, overweighted—like so many of our young writers—with a sense of his own responsibility towards life and art. He has no very obstinate theories upon social questions, no startling ideas about fiction. Writing to-day he can, of course, scarcely escape conscious craftsmanship, hardly avoid the discussion of marriage or sex. But he uses, and accepts, both as incidental to competent work. Being, above all things, a clever professional novelist, he has taken for atmosphere the spirit of his age, using it without pose or passion.

As already implied, Mr Beresford is, perhaps, most original in " God's Counterpoint." This is the story of an idealist, a Galahad among the quagmires of modernity. Philip Maning has strange, strict ideas about women; which, in fact, amount to mental disease or obsession. Inheriting from a savagely Puritan father elementary conceptions of sin, he mixes the old monastic conception of the " devil in women " with fanatic worship of the Woman. To him, all questions, or aspects, of sex were " thrust into one definite category, labelled ' beastliness.' He had no other word for it, and that one very well indicates his attitude. To him these things were unclean, and even at school he had begun to practise a fastidious cleanliness in his person."

Here, as indeed everywhere, he is morbidly oppressed by the sense of sin. A true Calvinist, he dreads all spontaneous emotion, which he calls a temptation of the Evil One. Unclean visions haunt his suppressed nature during the night hours, seriously disturbing his mental balance.

Only a strong character could have survived such a confusion of moral values. Luckily, Philip *is* strong; and, curiously enough, a man of imagination. In consequence, over the ordinary affairs of life he governs himself sternly, but remains attractive, and wears his unique " goodness " with charm. He is, in fact, really impressive—extorting affectionate respect; and the Holy of Holies whereinto he lifts good women shines fair and beautiful. They are, obviously, above sex.

After the preliminary home life, carefully analysed, Philip enters the world through the medium of a somewhat unusual publishing office. Robert Wing " saw literature in terms of ' what suited the public.' . . . It was his affair to provide ' pure ' literature for the millions who were sick and tired of eternal immorality." His pet authors did not proclaim or denounce. Their object " might be defined as the effort to prove that to be good was not necessarily to be dull." Himself a hypocrite, and personally sensuous, Wing naturally welcomed the amazing seriousness and sincerity of Philip as a business asset of great value. He believed, with all his soul, what the other professed. And the combination

J. D. BERESFORD

—with humorous interludes—worked well for a time.

Then our hero fell in love: or perhaps one should rather say—imagined that he had found the ideal woman. Evelyn naturally disapproved of his attitude towards her from the beginning, but loved him, trusting familiarity would make him normal. However, his firm shyness and delicate idealism remained unshaken, and all advances towards real intimacy and understanding came from her. Philip dreaded, first marriage itself, and then—more fastidiously—its consummation. Even when half convinced and yielding to the genuine love between them, he felt (or at least soon came to feel) that he had lowered his own ideal and degraded her. They were driven apart.

After which came, inevitably, spiritual collapse. Meeting the ordinary female butterfly, a creature of light passions and totally unmoral, Philip indulged infidelities which would never have tempted a more normal and healthy-minded loving husband.

But " only his body was scarred." The real Philip emerges once more; still an idealist but now also a man. This time he woos his wife humbly yet passionately; and she, being a woman, understands. Because now " he can teach her to love," she trusts the future.

If morbidity here be slightly strained or exaggerated, Mr Beresford redeems the fault by a fine optimism. Philip and Evelyn challenge and conquer fate by sheer courage and strong faith. It is a triumph of character, revealing the best possible to man. For once the perversities of introspection and self-analysis do not produce tragedy, because at bottom the man has a clean heart and a brave soul.

Dickie in "These Lynnekers" begins life with somewhat the same attitude. Sex seemed vaguely " shameful " to him as a boy; and " always, the confinement of a house had had the effect of presenting love in the shape of something to be despised and desperately fought against, something secret and unclean."

But such questions did not, for him, represent life as a whole; they seldom invaded his consciousness, and then quite incidentally. His pre-occupation was, rather, " holding his own " in the practical affairs of life, against the prevailing atmosphere of a curiously ineffective family type.

All the Lynnekers had charm—and prejudices. They were born to drift—pleasantly—towards disaster. They were "the County," and for them, always, " everything went on just the same." Only Dickie, and one of his sisters, were not like that. She married " unsuitably," and drifted to Canada; he, facing the world, saved the family—crowning success by a happy marriage.

Mr Beresford contrives his plot, however familiar its framework, with considerable ingenuity. His hero is a fine, healthy-minded personality : not quite typical, but yet fairly normal. His father and mother are dramatically contrasted, yet harmonious. They and the family all possess strongly-marked individuality. The novel, in fact, is thoroughly interesting, thoroughly competent; and every way an artistic achievement. But it does not invite detailed criticism.

Personally I am disposed to regard " The Jervaise Comedy " as a slighter effort in the same manner. We have here again a complacently " superior " family group; also disturbed by the " independence " of one member —here, a daughter, who insists on marrying the chauffeur. There is a touch of farce and melodrama in this episode, and though Melhuish, who tells the tale, claims to experience a " form of conversion " in his own love affair, no one troubles very seriously about his changed heart. This, in fact, is no more than a pleasant comedy, pleasantly planned, and well told.

It is permissible, maybe, to regard " The House in Demetrius Road " as one more study in genius and egoism. Greg, indeed, is not precisely an artist, at war with his own imagination, but he has—clearly enough—the potentialities of exceptional greatness and a commanding personality. He combines intimate charm with almost intolerable selfishness and aggressive discourtesy. He is the complete bully.

He is not, however, on ordinary occasions wholly responsible for his own words or deeds, being practically ruined by drink. A less dominating personality would have entirely collapsed before this story begins. It is concerned with the heroic attempt at cure by his secretary and his sister-in-law; two young people of spiritual enthusiasm who fall in love with each other at sight, but are prepared, in the event, for complete self-sacrifice in their devotion to a most thorny endeavour.

Mr Beresford has given us a very graphic picture of exaltation—following effort and hope, reaction—following failure and despair. The cure, in fact, is (for a time) thoroughly successful; but Greg's insane jealousy—at any division of allegiance—brings about the inevitable relapse, and the lovers are practically driven to desertion: holding that they have, after all, a right to happiness.

It would be difficult to imagine a horror revealed more dramatically; a character wasted more utterly; a sacrifice rewarded with more justice. The narrative carries conviction, and rivets our attention throughout.

We all, naturally, read Mr Beresford himself into the " Stahl " trilogy; and certain " confessions " of that hero regarding his literary career rather suggest that our novelist attaches particular importance to his essays in the " fantastic "; but I do not find " The Hampden-shire Wonder " at all convincing. Mr Beresford has been compared to " a man who has overcome a stammer," and so speaks with undue " precision and deliberateness . . . is almost too self-possessed."

In the interpretation of Victor Stott, the Wonder, the " stammer " has conquered him.

That incredible infant, whose intelligence o'ertops humanity in the ratio of some millions to one, and who knows everything, condescends occasionally, indeed, to interpret life, but always, to my mind, remains halting and obscure. Mr Beresford appears to be altogether lost among the philosophies. Really, he does not know what to do with the "Wonder" he has created; and ordinary mankind is far more interesting. Victor's father and mother, in fact, are really remarkable people. The pre-natal pre-occupations which are supposed responsible for the phenomenon, are ingeniously suggested, and their attitude towards their uncanny offspring is well thought out. But Victor, being inhuman, fails to interest the plain man. As Challis, the travelled philosopher, remarked: "Take my advice, leave him alone. . . . And meanwhile leave us our childish fancies, our little imaginings, our hopes—children that we are—of these impossible mysteries beyond the hills."

I have very much the same feeling about "The Goslings": though, obviously, the author intends here to present a philosophy of life. Having imagined that the whole of Europe (and to a lesser degree, also, America) is devastated by a terrible plague which carries off practically the whole male population, he describes for us a world of women, who are driven to nature for mere sustenance—literally earned by the sweat of their brow. They are also, inevitably, deprived of all protection or guidance from the habits and customs of civilisation, thrown back on their own initiative, and compelled to establish a new code of practical morality. Mr Beresford's sympathies are, it is clear, with those who welcome the change and have no yearnings after a return to the old order of things.

The occasion affords him an opportunity for several suggestive criticisms of convention, but as no reform of the social organism is likely to be affected by such means, I am, personally, not interested in the argument. It all seems in some way unreal, almost inhuman. It lacks even adventure.

Mr Beresford's slim volume of short stories called "Signs and Wonders" belongs to the same group, and reveals similar characteristics. The "Night of Creation," however, is an effective ghost-story if somewhat over-weighted with comment; and there is one suggestive and interesting, though purely conjectural, idea that recurs in all his most cryptic presentations of "other worlds," where "things happen" in the sky: "The people of that incredibly distant world, walking, as they always do, with their gaze bent upon the ground, are probably unable to see the signs and wonders that blaze across the sky. They, like ourselves, are so pre-occupied with the miserable importance of their instant lives."

This, I take it, variously expressed in Mr Beresford's different visions of the unseen, may be interpreted as a hint of purgatory. In other words, he would surmise, or suggest, that man is no more ready, after death than before, to realise the full Revelation; scarcely, in fact, more spiritual; still intent upon material trivialities. Though somewhat crudely illustrated, the theory has this justification; that it supports our hope of a gradual, and by no means complete, change through death; a *continuous* spiritual growth towards infinity. Yet the most daring, because most definitely dramatic, of these " guesses at truth," is also—without question—the most real and convincing. " The Miracle " offers a fine illustration of spirituality. Eager to reach the essential spirit personality of her dying husband, " poised out of time and space, away somewhere in the void," a wife finds herself wandering among wraiths of humanity, " peering vaguely downwards with bent head and eyes," till one moves " definitely towards her, drawn by the power of her longing." By her own effort she " would compel him to come with her." And " as she came slowly out of some remote distance to a realisation of herself," the " living dead man," given up by " all the specialists," was " sitting up in his bed . . . boastful to be alive again." Love triumphant cries : " I've brought you back, and I am going to hold you here." Mr Beresford has convinced us that so it was.

There are also, in this volume, several attempts at normal character-sketching, based on effects of the war; but they are, for the most part, too vague or general for edification. Like so many of his contemporaries, Mr Beresford is really hampered by the strength of isolated emotions, lacking aim or cohesion. They do not achieve either reasonable criticism or constructive purpose.

He would have spared us the careful record of George Wallace, who wrote a book " without having put pen to paper," had he remembered Henry James and the exquisite pathos of " The Madonna of the Future."

" Housemates," on the other hand, though written five years later than the second instalment of Jacob Stahl, reads almost like a " study " for that elongated autobiography. The hero, indeed —unlike Jacob—remains an architect : but superficially his apprenticeship is very similar, and his character develops along much the same lines. He is a hesitating, over-modest dreamer of dreams, prone to self-depreciation and self-analysis, yet conscious of power and, by fits and starts, given to startling self-assertion. He is, indeed, completed and dismissed with comparative brevity; but not, therefore, less fully realised or presented. After the usual beginning of a struggle with poverty, and a rude awakening to the complications of real life, he becomes most " unsuitably " engaged and, discovering his mistake, drifts into a boarding-house—where he meets his affinity. He is, as it were, more concentrated than Jacob. The one passion, which from the first proves itself true love, absorbs the man; takes him in hand, transfigures him.

Inwardly, " Housemates " is pure romance, and wholly satisfying as romance. The personalities of its hero and heroine are individual and strong. But its constructive details fall far below

Mr Beresford's usual standard. The minor characters are either commonplace or unreal; the incidents are dull, and Helen's grotesque attempt at supreme self-sacrifice in the cause of friendship strikes a thoroughly false note. It is sheer perverse cant.

We must, however, finally judge Mr Beresford from " The Early History of Jacob Stahl," " A Candidate for Truth," and " The Invisible Event." The hero himself develops into a successful novelist, the reviews quoted (in " The Invisible Event ") of his first book are taken verbatim from those which actually appeared of Jacob Stahl, and therefore his theories of fiction must be assumed the author's. These are mainly expressed in dialogue, or argument, with one Meredith, a fairly successful novelist whom Jacob admires, but criticises.

Meredith declares that modern " realism is not art . . . the realism of Dickens and his school consists, not in reporting the slang and cant phrases of the day, but in inventing a form of speech which shall definitely represent a type to the mind of the reader . . . the artist must bring something to his work, must define something more than a mere replica of his subject. He must express an attitude—the artist crystallises all the elements of an idea into one masterpiece. Nature never does that—not even in humanity."

On the other hand, Jacob wants " data, clearly defined premises; in life I want actuality, as a stimulus for my imagination. Give me correct drawing in a picture or in a novel, and I can work inwards or outwards—whichever it is—from that. But hazy outlines don't provide me with the material I'm looking for."

Elsewhere, Stahl consenting, Meredith proclaims the realist as one who does not " concentrate on the larger emotions—quite the reverse; he finds the common feelings and happenings of everyday life more representative. You may have a big scene, but the essential thing is the accurate presentation of the commonplace."

Jacob will not admit that life should be transmuted by the author's temperament, " translating all your impressions into a sort of phantasmagoria, a sort of general effect." He prefers putting a little piece of life, as he knows it, under the microscope, and not relating it to the whole; indifferent about whether " anything can come of it." Always he seeks to be realistic without being definite . . . to work it all out with the most convincing exactitude.

What, then, does Mr Beresford make of his realism; which is, certainly, a devotion to commonplace detail, though untainted—it seems —with any marked obsession on sex?

The three novels are, undoubtedly, built upon minute observation. They record the surface of life—with immense elaboration. We meet Jacob in a perambulator, and leave him " to face new beginnings " in his forty-first year. On broad lines his was not a particularly eventful life. He fails as an architect; succeeds, once he achieves concentration, as a novelist; has one early love affair, falls under the influence of a soul-fisherman, and marries twice. There are, in reality, few changes of scene, and not a long list of dramatis personæ, but everything moves with extreme deliberation, and is most thoroughly thought out. Jacob himself has a passion for comment, is very sensitive to impressions, and all is told through his mind.

So far, indeed, Mr Beresford conforms to the " new " realism. His observation is not confined to the surface, he does analyse thought. But he retains the method of the materialist, including a vast array of *facts* experienced, things *said*, action and furniture. He works on the old principle, from the outside.

From all which emerges, however, a very vivid, lifelike, and interesting personality. One may say that, with his touch of genius, Jacob is not abnormal. His eternal self-questionings do not kill charm, or even simplicity. Though always thinking and talking about himself, seeing all life and all people as they react on himself, we love the man. Contrary to all appearance, he has moral backbone. There, indeed, lies the secret.

Mr Beresford has shown us a weak creature; almost grotesquely unpractical, offensively modest, idly irresolute, selfishly egotistical. Easily captured by two impossible women, foolishly worshipping a plaster saint, he shuffles through a vast sea of misfortune, seemingly without aim or purpose, obviously destined to final, complete failure. We grow utterly weary, indeed, of his perpetual fumbling for something he calls himself.

Only the *real* Jacob was " ever at the beginning of life "; the very end of his long story is a new beginning; " virtue lies only in the renewal of effort." Five words—" you didn't think so once "—were the " epitome of his life." The mass of mankind regarded them as a reproof, he as high praise; and that was the essential difference.

In other words, he remained always a child, ready and eager for new ideas, new experience; willing to change. There is, indeed, some appearance of finality, or perhaps one would say fulfilment, in the third novel. Speaking according to convention, real love makes a man of him. When stimulated and steadied by the understanding and sympathy of Betty Gale, something real, strong, and unselfish comes to the surface. The vision materialises. We see then that Jacob was, all the while, not only seeking an ideal, but, after his queer fashion, living up to it. After all, the real man was essentially simple-minded, singularly affectionate, fundamentally spiritual. Vigour and will, too, were hidden, not killed.

Because she, too, had innate nobility, the woman accepted, proudly and happily, the last great test. For though she had raised him to both artistic achievement and material success, sure of no more backsliding, still he was not content. He must strive always; always change, develop, wonder, and search.

For still he "lacks sight of some definite, guiding motive that shall one day, he hopes, give form and purpose to the whole." He would still describe himself, in Emerson's words, as a "candidate for truth."

It is not, I take it, Mr Beresford's ambition to offer conclusions about life. Reproduction is his ideal; and the work is masterly. It is an absolutely true picture, very much alive, sincere, thorough, and sane.

There is, however, one issue wherein his passion for exact realism seems to have led him astray; and very possibly it is just this mistaken consistency which may account for a certain heaviness of manner in parts of the story which tries our patience. I have mentioned that Jacob Stahl was slow in thought, and hesitating in action. Nearly always, moreover, he found a difficulty in expressing himself. But Mr Beresford has set himself to write *through* Jacob. Therefore he, too, is perpetually fumbling for words, offering us all the stages by which Jacob first thinks of an idea; then doubts and questions it, finally making some half-dozen attempts to tell someone else about it, or put it in a book. We have, further, re-statements (often the final expression) from friend or wife; which he accepts or rejects.

In fact, Mr. Beresford has no scruple whatever against worrying out his thoughts on paper and letting us watch the process. "He can refine emotion until it becomes a fidget." Faith in the "letter" of realism injures some of his best work. Modern novelists, like the rich, talk too much.

He has returned, however, in " An Imperfect Mother " to the manner of " God's Counterpoint." Here there is no hesitation, no worrying over the analysis of a soul. Stephen, the hero, is a clearly conceived, well-defined character, at once resolute and sympathetic, fixed yet sensitive : true to type with a most marked outline. His " imperfect " mother is no less firmly drawn. In the beginning she had been everything to him—as he remained to her : only a certain waywardness of the artistic brilliancy in the woman baffled his direct youthfulness, and at the crisis of her life misunderstanding proved him inadequate. Then while he developed with rare moral courage and brain vigour to a fine maturity, she found life—as her folly made it—strangely hollow and unsatisfying.

Only where Stephen encountered fate in the person of a half-spoilt beauty wholely adorable, his mother again played providence to her handsome son. Claiming at first his undivided devotion, she came gradually to recognise that the most loving of chains can hold no man against his will. Then the imperfect one reached heroism. Putting aside all jealousy of youth seeking after youth, taking a back seat with seeming gaiety, she made the supreme sacrifice of helping him whom her heart yearned for as hers and hers only; to the attainment of what she knew would separate them for ever. Literally she gave him away.

"In future she would be—just his mother; a useful, elderly relation who was expected to be sympathetic and kind on all occasions; no doubt he would still be polite to her."

Up to a point the boy realised her self-sacrifice; but he could never understand *why* she wanted more than he was ready to give. Her final attitude seemed to him just right. She was " going to be sensible " : that was his summary of the affair.

Wherefore because he loved wisely, because his lady, for all her imperious frivolity, admired the " man," they took and held the great gift of love. Joy to youth, sorrow for age, is Mr Beresford's conclusion; and it is reached here through a fine record of average humanity. There is not even the slight strain towards the abnormal we found in " God's Counterpoint," and yet the characters are perfectly individual, thoroughly alive, and unusually attractive.

I am disposed to think that the story pleases one so entirely, in part because it is in a sense so ordinary. There is no search after subtlety, no superfluity of wonder, no startling discoveries about man's soul. This is not, indeed, Mr Beresford himself looking out at us, giving himself away. He had to *go inside* these people : to observe them, study their personality. But on the other hand he was not misled by appearances, he " got " there. He has given us, in fact, no superficial realism; but a chapter of truth about men and women.

" Revolution " has an especially profound

interest for the present generation. Mr Beresford has here revealed, with sincere conviction, one striking aspect of the effects that experience of the trenches may produce on a sensitive soul. Paul Leaming is, most literally, " possessed " by one idea, one spiritual endeavour, to which he is ready to sacrifice even his own honour. He will, so far as his influence may be strained to extend, prevent bloodshed, subdue the desire to kill, replace violence by brotherly love. He has seen the blood-lust, he knows how easily men slip back into the savage—once they have handled death; torn, or seen others tear, into human flesh. The vision of what may be, once evil passions prevail, haunts his imagination, day and night, as some ghastly nightmare.

Wherefore he thinks, feels, and acts—almost as Christ taught; is what Tolstoy would have us be. To afford occasion for his overmastering gospel, Mr Beresford imagines that English Labour has actually achieved—what the reactionaries are always whispering it desires and, if not crushed, will accomplish: overthrown the government, secured the army, repudiated the constitution, set up Soviets. Obviously, the " Revolution " begets violence. Paul is spurred to give expression to the faith that is in him. He does not at first, indeed, tackle the whole nation, plead with humanity at large. But in his own small village; where he can influence the Lord of the Manor, and can—in some measure—spiritualise the yokels; he instantly plans, preaches, and —for a time—evolves an almost complete, Tolstoyan community. He abolishes (in one small English parish not easily approached from the outer world) private property, distributes food through a democratically elected committee, and revives something approaching the mediaeval.

Soldiering, however, had produced different effects upon the brutal villager who leads the revolutionaries; and Paul is not quick enough to prevent him murdering the hot-headed Mr Leaming, senior, and one other obstinate farmer, whom no reasoning will convince. Only because the Idealist will neither punish nor revenge; since he is ready to let God judge even Jem Oliver; offering brotherhood over his father's corpse; the " miracle " happens.

This is a daring, very suggestive, and most truthful, imaginative feat. Paul's character is drawn with patient, unfaltering intensity. One only hopes that many who have shared his experiences may feel like him, and be able—should similar tests arrive—to prove equally heroic. This is the one lesson worth learning from Armageddon, the one faith all should proclaim with the holy passion of inspired conviction.

I am not sure, however, if Mr Beresford has not rather weakened the force of his message by other traits prominent in Paul. He is one, we read, who had been long mentally paralysed by shell-shock. He has a habit of falling into a sort of trance; losing control of himself, not seeing or hearing what is happening to those around him. At such times he realises the mystic meanings of Nature, yearns towards abstract beauty, and gains spiritual confidence, hope for man, and a new faith in God. This may well be the natural soul-complement of his Tolstoyan mind, but accompanied, as we find it, by a lapse to physical inertia and mental groping, it certainly provokes the philistine comment that, after all, Paul is not quite sane : " a dear, fine fellow—but just a little —you know." All of which, to my mind, lessens the great value of what Mr Beresford, I presume, has here set out to teach.

In the closing chapters, a counter-revolution is manœuvred, and the reactionaries bring back the old order : using methods of drastic revenge, wholesale shooting, and what we have learnt to call " reprisals "—which, even among his own people, Paul could not prevent. He is roused, at last, to a sense of national responsibility ; and Mr Beresford leaves him full of hope, bound for London " to form a society or something." He had not lost faith in the vision : " he must spend himself in the love of his own kind ; and in doing that he must surely express his certainty that the salvation of every living being was finally assured. For was not every man and woman his spiritual equal, and was not he himself assured of some ultimate transfiguration by which he would break the bonds of a physical confinement ? "

Once more, I feel, Mr Beresford suffers from not having made up his own mind. He cannot, himself, realise his hero's vision. The problem, the situation, is stated with vigour and truth, far more so as regards its influence on varied types than I have here space to indicate. But, like all the moderns, he cannot really see his way out, he has no clear conception of a new world, not even a certain sense of its aim or direction.

Probably, " The Convert " (in " Signs and Wonders ") is a " study " for this prophecy; though, curiously enough, its actual plot-structure is almost identical with that of Mr Cannan's " Pugs and Peacocks." The scholar-hero of both novelists is shaken out of himself by a world-upheaval, that, destroying his " whole life's work," robs him of " every happiness and satisfaction he ever had." In both cases the brilliant " back-number " steps down boldly to face realities, " hand-in-hand with creative youth "—in the person of a charming, though downright girl-reformer.

" The Prisoners of Hartling," closely recalling Demetrius Road, belongs to Mr Beresford's small group of achievements, and need not be added to his more voluminous experiments.

THE EARLY HISTORY OF JACOB STAHL	1911
THE HAMPDENSHIRE WONDER	1911
A CANDIDATE FOR TRUTH	1912
THE GOSLINGS	1913
THE HOUSE IN DEMETRIUS ROAD	1914
THE INVISIBLE EVENT	1915
MOUNTAINS OF THE MOON	1915
THESE LYNNEKERS	1916
HOUSEMATES	1917
NINETEEN IMPRESSIONS	1918
GOD'S COUNTERPOINT	1918
THE JERVAISE COMEDY	1919
AN IMPERFECT MOTHER	1920
REVOLUTION	1921
SIGNS AND WONDERS	1921
THE PRISONERS OF HARTLING	1922

D. H. LAWRENCE

Mr D. H. Lawrence is far more of his own generation as a poet not only in verse, than as narrator or in construction. His aggressive realism drags through deeper and blacker mud than the most morbidly decadent of " problem " protests that Victorianism ever evoked. He over-emphasises and perverts sex, in obstinate blindness to human nature : after the manner of earlier realists.

Yet his Vision of Man, crushed or uplifted by real communion with Nature, reveals, with a fine and sensitive art, that almost new Reading of Earth, which Hardy suggests and the Georgians have made their own. This is far, indeed, from the flower-painting of either Wordsworth or Tennyson, their tale of God in a primrose or in the brook. It does not reveal, or depend on, minute knowledge or a keen eye. Pictorially it is pure impressionism, a thing of blob and splash; black shadow-deeps, hot sun-rays, and rank smells. It utters a mood, never a thought. The poets to-day write in a strange tongue of their Mother Earth and of animal or plant life : cursing the stains of soil, or as lovers exulting to be sod-bound.

The little weakness for talking of Shaw and Swinburne, of Wagner or Verlaine in cowsheds and coalmines, should prove easy to outgrow. Self-respect, surely, will cure so sound an artist of such cheap smartness of phrase as " boys and girls pairing off for the after-chapel stroll and spoon," or " she used to go the whole hogger," and of the now popular jerk-style : " Heads or tails. Then tails. See the poetic justice."

Mr Lawrence, despite ugly phrasing and strained analysing, interprets " the Country " with deep insight and dramatic power. All spiritual abstractions, translating the Voice of God, lie outside his ken; but the farm-life of " White Peacock," for instance, reaches far beyond mere observation, the trick technique of local colour. Nature speaks through the family in the home. " The Father," primitive, cheery, and elemental, scarcely aware of men and things outside his home-paddock; the quiet " lady of the house "; and Emily, " the serious-minded," with her shy nibbles at culture, her sad grace, and her retiring yet resolute self-sufficiency. And, above all, George himself, poet and brute. " You think rather quiet folks have a lot in them, but it's only stupidity—they are mostly fools," said the imperious Lettie : voicing a spiteful half-truth. In the end, certainly, George proved himself a *great* fool; and he was always tongue-tied. He could neither find, nor express, himself amidst the high-brow chatter and short-hand subtleties of his best friends.

An upstanding youth, strong if blundering, in

natural egoism and a conceit of his own body; a truly magnetic force. A personality that pulls. It is, of course, an old story enough; the fascination of the primitive male for semi-sophisticated and spoiled beauty. Mr Lawrence seems to imply indeed that, had George been rather more of a brute, grasped and struck at the divinity he half worshipped and half despised, she would have gladly come to him—"like a barbarous woman, a slave." He could dominate her in the delirious dance, subdue her beside the plough; but quick words, or, above all, light laughter, stripped him of all manhood, and struck the yokel dumb.

This half-formed, tragically mixed specimen of humanity is real flesh and blood. Mr Lawrence reveals the earth-man, strangely sensing, but not tuned to, the finer issues of human thought. Nature has given him imagination and a soul; but in a vision without words. He has no language for a higher self; no experience or mental training to adjust soul-conflicts; no balance to steer life. No highly-strung, temperamental, and thoroughly modern girl could resist playing with such a fire: frank experiment in heart-breaking is the order of the day. And Lettie is no mere type.

Mr Lawrence, in fact, here achieves drama, at once human and sincere. The creatures of his imagination are so strongly felt, conceived by such true instinct, and interpreted with such fine art, as to conquer us despite the author himself. We are, in the end at least, so captured and absorbed as to accept, though not to believe or forgive, the fierce and crude heat of phrase—the needless bodily contact—the unclean musing of minds diseased. They seem to belong more to the author than to his work: they weakened, but for a time failed to kill, his art.

So it is with "Sons and Lovers," even a bigger triumph in the same mood. He has here borrowed, and developed, a morbid perversion from "Jude the Obscure"; but, for all her "imported" falseness, Miriam is a true woman when herself. The supreme tragedy of a nature over-developed in one respect, to whom inheritance and fate deny full self-understanding, who can never—for that reason—be or give completely and of her best, has seldom been drawn with such intense power. Almost the great Earth-spirit, mother and lover in one, she is yet too human, and broken in her humanity, for the triumph of the divine, that could alone have brought real manhood to quivering, soul-tortured Paul. But, incomplete, she towers immeasurably over her mere sex-rivals; in charm, substance, and depth.

Paul was obviously born to trouble, and we have no quarrel with Mr Lawrence for his moral instability, divided allegiance, and ignoble surrender to the spirit of female allure; here personified with all the sure touch and quasi-subtlety we expect from the moderns. It is here the Man for whom Nature and Civilisation fight "to the death": a battle-field that is at once more dramatic, more varied and finished, of deeper human significance, than Strelley Mill.

This, too, is only a part of " Sons and Lovers." Mrs Morel, Paul's mother, dominates him and the whole book. In herself, and in her relation to the plot, she may be said to stand with those two other great fiction mothers—from Mrs Mordaunt's " The Pendulum " and Miss Reeve's " Helen in Love." Pride, tyranny, stern self-suppression, secret ambition and a very passion of love may be found in all three. Paul's sense of motherhood, too, was no less strongly and deeply developed, or less instinctive, than Michael Saerre's. For both she was Home, and home so frequently would contract or kill life.

Mr Lawrence has a big subject here, and he handles it with power and distinction. Always deep down in the very roots of nature the mother stands first with Paul. He is loyal, indeed, against extreme provocation to disloyalty; not so much, perhaps, from her personality, as from the hard tangle of sordid poverty, a horrible Mr Morel, and all the brothers and sisters one would expect, each with an exacting vitality of their own, more or less mutually destructive to free development of personality. For him, indeed, they are of little account, save as in various ways, at different times, they come between mother and son : the ruling motive of life.

We may read two judgments from " Sons and Lovers "; and Mr Lawrence nowhere dictates our choice. Mrs Morel may be held to have killed Paul's manhood, as she hampered his growth : so that he just missed the power to rule life or himself, and achieve complete individuality. She may, on the other hand, be honoured as the one real thing in his life, at once the foundation and the support of a character, which, wandering, and stirred by other loves, could but, at last, return to home.

Either way hers is a vital, arresting personality in the centre of a life-like picture of active, intense emotion among the colliers of its author's boyhood.

It is on these two novels Mr Lawrence must so far rest. Both are distinguished by vivid emotion, strong characterisation, and a vein of true poetic imagination.

Elsewhere the faults, obvious enough even in them, have almost completely obscured a far less virile art. " The Trespasser " moves in such narrow limits that its characters are dwarfed out of all nature : its poetic beauty yields to morbid pre-occupations. The minute aim defeats its own subtlety. It is the psychology of an atom, a riot of passion in so small a compass, that only noise and fury can explode. To " The Rainbow " belongs the unenviable distinction of justifying censorship. It is not only all wrong, but a bad art.

In the volume of short stories called " A Prussian Officer " the morbid descriptions of " physical contact," sexual inarticulate cries, hot flames and long males, destroy any pleasure one might derive from the rather ordinary plots and crude characterisation. We cannot accept these " fierce virgins " who hunger after nakedness.

There is some compensation, however, in "The Lost Girl." It opens, indeed, in its author's worst manner. The experiments in life with which Alvina breaks loose are as impossible to the girl she is meant to be as any of Ursula Trent's,[1] and told with even more vulgarity. She flounders among men without even the justification of quick impulse or strong passions. Her "mental friendship" with Mr May, however, is sane and sound enough; and almost from that episode the book steadies down. The American, with his characteristic "sort of private innocence," is a man. It is reasonable and true, moreover, for Alvina, "withering towards old-maiddom," to hate "independence" and take on "the big well-to-do man of fifty-three" for a "very nice home and lovely things in it." We can well believe that "she was as fussy as if someone had given her a lovely new pair of boots."

Yet in the end Cicio was bound to prevail. Mr Lawrence means something quite real and well-conceived in this almost wordless Italian and his magnetic personality. Here, again, the thought is expressed with an unclean violence that must repulse. Only its strength and sincerity break through verbiage. The people are so right, all they feel and say so wrong.

Alvina did *not* " moan in spirit " or " feel dead in his arms." Cicio did not " kiss her with a passionate finesse that seemed like coals of fire on

[1] By W. L. George.

her head." There was no occasion for her to be " an obscure woman, as if she was veiled," or feel like " a sacred prostitute." No kind of love means " beautiful, cool loneliness " that can, at the same time, " invade " or " extinguish " a woman and " send her unconscious."

Yet there was real love, we are convinced, between these two. Mr Lawrence cannot see clearly what he himself has made. It was a rare experience, not the highest of course, but of strength and depth to endure. After his own way, not without its charm, the man drew Alvina out of her insincerities, roused her life; and *for her* did what, probably, no other influence, more *or* less virile, could have done so well. Poor and solitary in his miserable village home, he " revered her because she was with child "; and the implied bond in sacred responsibility is not a *small* ideal.

Mr Lawrence then, we believe, had once great gifts of a creative imagination built on poetry and art. Yet he was doomed to fail—in two ways; through overmastering sex-obsession and total lack of ideas. He could not see life from more than one angle, and he saw so little of life. He has only expressed his own fiery moods and obscured vision. He has not thought, or listened, or looked.

Unfortunately " Women in Love " proves only too clearly that he has succumbed to the former, and more deadly, alternative. He has here sacrificed even the small modicum of art and vision that he permitted himself in " The Rainbow,"

D. H. LAWRENCE

and lost his soul for the convulsive revelation of " the strange and magical current of force in a man's back and loins, and down his legs; force so perfect that it stayed him immobile and left his face subtly, mindlessly, smiling." This, he cries, is " the basic mind, the deepest physical mind "; from which we derive " a pure and magic control, magical, mystical, a force in darkness, like electricity."

Under the influence of the mindless mind, which ordinary folk call madness, the characters of this terrible sex-explosion are either " negated " or " fulfilled "; they are " polarised," or they " lapse out." Their " inchoate, absolved " eyes, " suspended " bodies, and " suave loins of darkness," lead one couple to know " the great dreadful mysteries." While Hermione, " her heart a pure flame in her breast," finds " pure unconsciousness " in the " ecstasy " of murder: and Gerald's " body jolted, his heart had burst into flame," as " a blinding flash went over his brain."

Unfortunately such ravings as these mean something fundamental to Mr Lawrence. Unless he can release his artistic powers from their " sound, and fury " we must but lament our loss.

THE WHITE PEACOCK	-	1911
SONS AND LOVERS	-	1913
THE TRESPASSER -	-	1914
A PRUSSIAN OFFICER	-	1914
THE RAINBOW	-	-
THE LOST GIRL -	-	1920
WOMEN IN LOVE -	-	1921

COMPTON MACKENZIE

MODERN criticism has decided that, for all his outspoken revelations of the underworld, Mr Compton Mackenzie is essentially romantic. He does not, in fact, see life as it is, but as he desires it to be; that is, as it will best illustrate the characters of his imagination, best occupy the light splendour and swift precision of his most opulent vocabulary. As he says of his own Michael, even his conception of irregularity is essentially romantic. He has invented London and peopled it with marionettes. Maybe the fact should not diminish our admiration as, certainly, it cannot decrease our enjoyment. The credit is all his own; he is quite irresistible. The keen vitality of his work, its sublime self-confidence, its youth, its colour and its movement, positively forbid reflection. We forgive the melodrama and condone the hysteria. The swift rush of ideas carry us captive; the brilliant pictures intoxicate; the narrative marches triumphant through a thousand fine threads—crossing each other again and again, darting hither and thither, yet never knotted or ravelled, ragged or in confusion, never broken in loose ends.

Superficially Mr Mackenzie reveals many of the characteristics we associate with his realistic contemporaries. As we have already implied, he calls a spade a spade. Ugly words and unsavoury material do not frighten him. He spares us no detail of what is offensive to ears polite.

With a passion for detail, moreover, he spreads himself over the minutiæ of existence; spinning out volume after volume concerning the same persons or group of persons, with infinite patience and—apparently secure against boredom. He has told us as much or more about Michael and Sylvia, as Mr Beresford has narrated of Jacob Stahl: there seems no reason why he should not achieve the final completeness of Miss Richardson. "Are a thousand pages too long," he cries, "for the history of twenty-five years of man's life? That is to say if one holds, as I do hold, that childhood makes the instrument, youth tunes the string, and early manhood plays the melody." "I very much doubt," says one of his heroes, "if any impressions after eighteen or nineteen help the artist. All experience after that age is merely valuable for maturing and putting into proportion the more vital experience of childhood."

Here is a theory which may explain why so many of our novelists to-day devote so many chapters to the schooldays of their heroes, after voluminous reflections from the nursery. Indeed, starting from Mr Waugh's "Loom of Youth," we could easily construct an educational encyclopedia from contemporary fiction, which should be profoundly interesting and instructive. If Mr Mais cannot forget that he was once a schoolmaster, the others—with triumphant accuracy—can recall their schooldays. There is, of course, much to be said for the importance and influence of our surroundings in youth; but personally I am rather disposed to regard this particular obsession in fiction as no more than one example, among many, of that straining for over elaboration in analysis which is the last word in the old realism. Most young people are far more simple and less sensitive than our novelists would have us believe.

The whole first volume of " Sinister Street " carries Michael no further from home than St James, through chapters of a " preparatory " to the threshold of " dreaming spires." It includes, certainly, his early infatuation for Lily Haden, " when her arm was twined round him like ivy, and their two hands came together like leaves," and the awful discovery that she was quite ready to flirt with anybody. " But he was still only a schoolboy, an awkward lout of eighteen."

The question remains—how far do such voluminous minutes reveal character or reflect life? Are we or are we not more ready to understand and sympathise with the man, because we know so much of his nurse and governess, so many of his school-fellows? I would not reject childhood as in itself an unsuitable subject for fiction: but a clear impression of the general atmosphere, with any episode or incident that marked a crisis, would serve perfectly well as an interpretation of what this elongated narrative has been designed to preface : the character it unfolds.

Mr Mackenzie indeed reveals considerable sympathy with young people, and the tenaciousness of his memory is a marvel. " You know," says his Epilogical letter, " that if I were to set down all I could remember of my childhood the work would not yet have·reached much beyond the fifth year." He understands their attitude towards the foolish gaiety of the adult; he remembers how he once " supposed that to excite notice was the worst sin anyone could commit." He can still see " that golden head upon his shoulder," still feel curiosity stimulated by the abominable revelations of Brother Aloysius, or hear the voice of the " true decadent, treading delicately over the garnered perfection of the world's art," imaging its " abstract of humanity's immeasurable vice, while feminine devils put on tights and openwork stockings, to encounter him from the pages of pink weekly papers." The friendships and the jealousies, the ambitions and the rebellions, of the schoolroom are as fresh in his mind as to-day's paper. He knows that youth can be at once sublimely generous, horribly hard, and extravagantly sentimental; by turns humble, conceited, daring in originality, or slavish in imitation.

So at the close of his last autumn term, Michael found himself with a surer foothold on the rock-hewn foundations of truth. " He had disposed of whatever question, or action, or reaction, or reason, or contemplation, survived the destruction he was dealing out to the litter of idols, which he thought he had already destroyed, when he had merely covered them with a new coat of gilt."

But phases and experiences like these are common to boyhood; they do not particularly concern this particular specimen of the race.

There are, indeed, many attractive qualities in this volume. It does give us more than we meet elsewhere of his pathetic mother and of Stella, that wonderful sister of his, who declares " when I tell myself something very solemnly I must be speaking the truth." The horrible history by Meats (or Brother Aloysius) of his parents, explains the man as we meet him in later volumes. The teaching : " Be always a Don Quixote, however much people may laugh. It really means just being a gentleman "; gives us a clue to Michael's whole character; as he later declares that the word " gentleman " should mean more nowadays than it did in the past, since every generation should add something to its value.

Volume II takes us to Oxford, and though Michael complains at first that " the freshmen herd together in the dimensions of a school treat," so that he feels " more like a tourist than a Varsity man "; though he is bored to tears by half the men he goes about with; it all comes to have some real meaning for him in time, and does actually, in some sense, create the man. Here he acquires personality and an ego, though always remaining addicted to crude generalisations, and the profitless examination of his own soul. We may not be all snobs; but " it *is* convenient always to like the right people." Civilisation must have some power, or we should all revert. Oxford will change the Rhodes scholars much more profoundly than the Rhodes scholars will change Oxford—it will "cure them of being surprised by themselves or of showing surprise at anyone else"; at present they are "just as much barbarians as any freshman."

Some of his best friends, however, "were never sent into this world to puzzle out things." As he tells one of them, "you were sent here to sprawl across it, just as you're sprawling across that sofa. When you go down, you will go into the Egyptian Civil Service, and you'll sprawl over the Sahara in exactly the same way. I rather wish I were like you. It must be quite comfortable to sit down heavily and unconcernedly on a lot of people. I can't imagine a more delightful notion; only I should feel them wriggling under me." Which epitomises Imperialism.

Finally the "Oxford mixture" turns Michael into a good hater. He aspires to "all sorts of fanciful private beliefs," but wants to force everything within the Conventions. "I hate free thought, free love, and free verse, and yet I hate almost equally the stuffy people who have never contemplated their merit."

He "is rather fed up with toleration, really." However, young men will talk. The real Michael, whom Mr Mackenzie sets out, so patiently yet so riotously, to construct for us, must not be taken very seriously as a philosopher, even in cap and gown; though chivalrous by instinct, a dreamer easily fired to romance, he has a fine zest for life. He gains something from all men, much from a few : enjoying that which provokes criticism, following one line after another, always intent on pastures new. For him the " muddle of existence " never made existence itself less glorious. Roulette or polo, bloods or intellectuals, art or religion, misty twilights or autumn afternoons, being " just in time to make a tremendous noise "; or " jovial dinners where rowing men sat gigantically round the table and ate gigantically and laughed gigantically." These were Oxford : these he grasped heartily with both hands, drank of deeply with a will.

Still, even here and now, the man himself lived somewhat apart. As in schooldays, he had grown up essentially through the more varied and independent experience of holiday time, so it is not, after all, at the university itself that the completed personality stands forth. College life, college friends, varied and stimulating as they may be, seem after all but as the sowing of the seed.

Mr Mackenzie is taking us back, through bewildering bypaths, to the " Down underneath," as he pictures it; leading, curiously enough, through the exhibition gardens at Earls Court, to the " spectral reality of the Seven Sisters Road," and " the fetid population that thronged it "; their rooms " all much alike with their muslin and patchoulie, their aspidestras and yellowing photographs; as in unseen basements children whined, while on the mantelpiece garish vases rattled to the vibration of the traffic—unknown London with all its sly and labyrinthine romance."

After Oxford, indeed, Michael drifted somewhat till Chance or Fate once more showed him (in " a damnable place ") his Lily of the flower-soft kisses; seemingly driven into the oldest of all professions; and in him was born Don Quixote. She had vanished again, and, seized with the wholly fantastic idea that his early wooing made him responsible for her present circumstances, he plunges into the quest for Lily, and we are tossed without ceremony, full hilt into the atmosphere which Mr Mackenzie exploits, with all his passion for gaudy detail, in most of his later novels. Another coincidence meanwhile provides our hero with the best of all possible guides to this ugly world. He knocks up against Meats or Brother Aloysius—now known as Barnes; who at the outset assures him that all the differences he may observe between " under and upper " society arise solely from money—" Give me ten pounds a week and I could be a bloody angel . . . the man who first called poverty holy ought to be walking about hell with donkey's ears on his knob."

Michael is now determined to find Lily, and marry her; but Mr Mackenzie is not restrained by any similar determination to concentrate. He has " a jolly conception of the adventurous men of London," and puts no reins on his imagination. Michael now alternates between the most violent extremes of " gay life," gold tipped or dead drab. Author and hero alike seem powerless to resist or conceal their enjoyment of such many coloured experience, however eager and serious the missionary character of its occasion. Without for one moment desisting from his fevered search after Lily Haden, Michael permits himself to investigate, with alert thoroughness, the innermost miseries of mean streets; to cultivate a brisk irresponsible friendship with " shrewd, mirthful, kind, honest Daisy," the natural light of love, " immemorial in the scheme of the universe," with her " white dress and candid roguery "; to talk sympathetically with women like Mrs Smith " creeping about the stairs like spiders " : he is at home in luxurious flats, in brilliant ballrooms, in cafés and promenades.

When Lily is found, and after difficulties not of *her* making, persuaded to accept him, Michael once more fancies himself madly in love, quickly drops his quixotisms, and plays the devout lover to perfection. Wherefore when she (being, in fact, " doomed from the creation of the universe to be a plaything of man ") proved faithless to him on the very eve of marriage, he gives up " trotting round operating on the motes of other people," for the most serious consideration of " the beam in his own eye."

He may become a Benedictine monk : he may become a society preacher. Mr Mackenzie explains that these novels are not " a life, but the prologue of a life. He is growing up on the last page, and for us his interest begins to fade."

Can we, who have read " Sylvia and Michael," accept the sincerity of this assertion ? Sylvia, at any rate, exerts great influence upon the closing chapters of " Sinister Street," and I am unwilling to believe that the interpretation given in later novels of her conduct at this time was an afterthought, or that Mr Mackenzie could introduce such a strikingly original character into the fringe, as it were, of his narrative, without having already some conception, however fragmentary and unformed, of her past and future.

It would not, indeed, be unreasonable to call the " Early Life and Adventures of Sylvia Scarlett " a sequel to " Sinister Street "; except that Mr Mackenzie, instead of taking up his characters where he left them, goes back to his heroine's ancestry and childhood, leads her with great detail to the first meeting, and struggle for Lily, with Michael, and finally carries them both a few years forward. Michael, however, is once more left " engaged in saving his own soul."

Here for atmosphere we begin where " Sinister Street " left off; since whereas Michael was born more or less in the purple, Sylvia sprang most literally from the gutter. Here we see everything through the woman's eye, and from below upwards, not down from the Quixote platform. Whether in youth or maturity Sylvia was always the most vital centre of her surroundings. All the cool daring of her shrewd philosophy never drove her outside life, however sordid its colouring, however thankless its rewards. Taking right hold of everyone and everything—good, bad, or indifferent—she was always in full swing; tilting at all and sundry; sure of herself even when least aware of the consequences. Entering London in girlhood, under the protection of that hardened and yet irresolute criminal, her father, Sylvia has no moral guidance of any sort, no instructed conventions, no standard in thought or conduct; only sublime courage, enjoying candour, and an unerring instinct towards higher things.

Always and everywhere meeting with knocks and shocks, she yet miraculously contrives both to hit out in turn and to discover most of the fairest and gayest possibilities of human nature. After her own fashion, like Michael himself, she has a passion for lost causes; and, with untiring energy and unsparing self-sacrifice, always champions the weak and tender.

In the Brompton cemetery, she had the fancy to invent her own epitaph : *Here lies Sylvia who was always running away;* and that, indeed, was her invariable remedy for an impasse. Finding herself, as she did often enough, confronted with someone or something quite impossible, or entirely repulsive, she did promptly and positively run—without the slightest consideration of where she was going, what she could do next, how she could find the means merely to live. Knowing not fear, she would take up with anybody, try them by tests all her own, and act in strict accordance with the results. Once she took a charming boy with her, but he, lacking courage for the adventure, failed her then ; only

to reappear at an emotional crisis, win her
affections through the mother instinct in her, and
then, once more, vanish into the arms of " a funny
little red-haired girl." " Well, you know the
way things happen on tour." Which was the
end of her " Early Life and Adventures." For
the most part, however, making many friends
and more admirers, Sylvia contrived to enjoy life;
though there were terrible periods of the abyss.

She adored " the nightmare effect of London,
the sensation of being hopelessly plunged into a
maze of streets from which there's no escape. I
was plunged just like that into London. It is
gloriously and sometimes horribly mad, and
that's all I want."

Her brief experience of conventional marriage
with the first gentleman she ever met held its
happy moments; for Richard Iredale, if both
rigid and obtuse, had really broadminded
sympathies; only they had " different standards
of honour."

Wherefore she sold her body to save her soul,
and eleven years later she asked the priest in the
Confessional: " Can you understand that?
For three months I mortified my flesh by being
a harlot. Can you possibly understand the
deliberate infliction of such a discipline; not to
humiliate one's pride, but to exalt it? Can you
understand that I emerged from that three
months' incredible horror with a complete personality? I was defiled; I was degraded; I was
embittered; I hated mankind; I vowed to
revenge myself on the world; I scoffed at love;

and yet now when I feel that I have at last brushed from myself the last speck of mud that was still clinging to me, I feel that somehow all that mud has preserved me against a more destructive corruption. This does not mean that I do not repent of what I did, but can you understand how without a pride that could lead me to such depths, I could not have come through humility to a sight of God."

Not only her own experience, but that of the chorus girls and gay women, with whom so much of her life was spent (and their attitude towards life), made Sylvia at times very bitter, particularly towards men.

" Life is a nightmare. After all, what is life for me? Strange doors in strange houses, strange men and strange intimacies. Sometimes weirdly grotesque and incredibly beastly. The secret vileness of human nature flung at me. Man revealing himself, through individual after individual, as utterly contemptible. I tell you, my dear eager fool, it is beyond my conception ever to regard a man as higher than a frog, as less repulsive. So, I worship woman, and in this nightmare city, in this nightmare life, Lily was always beautiful; only beautiful, mind you. I don't want to worship anything but beauty. I don't care about purity or uprightness, but I must have beauty."

After the early adventures, Mr Mackenzie deserts his beloved and bewildering London for the still more garish and variegated Bohemia of the continent, in " Sylvia and Michael." Being so suddenly deserted " there was nothing else for Sylvia but to run away," " because whenever she had been brought face to face with a difficult situation she had run away "—though not previously out of England. Now in Paris, in Petrograd, wherever means are offered for women to empty the pockets of foolish or brutal pleasure-seekers, Sylvia runs the gauntlet of European depravity. Never accepting in its entirety the ugly terms of the life in which she appears to play so brilliant a part, she has, nevertheless, on the whole an exceedingly bad time; and, during periods of semi-starvation, touches depths to which all her experience of London had never driven her. Once more placed, by her enthusiastic devotion to girlhood, in an utterly false position; always alert to help a friend or even a mere acquaintance without regard to her own risk; finally caught in the tangle imposed by the Great War upon women in enemy countries, without any visible, recognised means of subsistence; she is, indeed, perilously near defeat.

But in the end, following that phase of stern self-criticism and mystical piety indicated by the extract already quoted from her confession, she finds, with Michael, two months of the most perfect companionship possible for human beings, " living between a blue sky and a blue sea." These are, indeed, " days of war," she sighs with desperate apprehension—" yet somehow, oh, my dearest and dearest and dearest, I don't believe I shall *lose* you."

One would suppose now that Mr Mackenzie had positively finished with these people, but in " The Vanity Girl " (1920) he unexpectedly reverts to certain of Sylvia's early theatrical experiences; leaving *her*, indeed, in the background, but also illustrating her from another's point of view. This method of throwback, chronologically speaking, is apt to confuse the reader, but he is himself never obscure or in doubt.

The main theme of the book centres round Dorothy Lonsdale (or Caffyn), originally neighbour and friend to Lily Haden. Who, finding her family suburban, and very much aware of her beauty, storms the stage. As a touring chorus girl, she shares lodging with Lily and Sylvia, and later with Olive Fanshaw. Having some very remote family connection with Bertie Lonsdale (known to Michael at Oxford) she attracts and captivates his friend, Lord Clarehaven.

This is a study of a girl absolutely concentrated on her own advancement. She is entirely devoid of morality, kindliness, or affection, but on the other hand, fired by passion and imagination in her devotion to Blue Blood. " If *you* don't realise what you owe to your name, I do," is her frequent reproach to her irresponsible husband; as, indeed, she does. Having succeeded in holding him off, without diminishing her attractiveness, till the Dowager was on her knees to the popular actress, she displayed the most shrewd discretion in her new sphere, quickly and easily taking the lead in the county. Then comes her 'Vision of the Heir,' who, after the infinite solicitude of her preparations, was sacrificed to save her life. "You don't suppose," cried Clarehaven, "I could have lived with a cursed child who had killed you."

He grows reckless, flouts her control, and loses heavily on cards and horses. The estates are hopelessly mortgaged, and at last sold outright to a rascally Jew in love with her ladyship. At the last moment, Dorothy—grown desperate—offers herself in exchange; is accepted, but, by accident, saved the consequences, since—war intervenes. Clarehaven is soon killed, but the Jew remains in possession.

Now, Dorothy *has* a son, wherefore she once more bargains. These are her terms: "Make over the old home, all the estate, to my son, and I will marry you. Being half-brothers or half-sisters to Lord Clarehaven will be honour enough for your children."

The ideal may be perverse, but it involves a supreme sacrifice. Here is no thought of self. She had schemed and planned and worked for position, without conscience, without remorse; she was ruthless to her own friends and her own family. But having attained, self is wiped out, merged in "The Family." There would be, indeed, no struggle, no conflict of desires on her part, but, thwarted at every turn by the husband who cares for nothing beyond the gratification of the moment, she fights, sacrifices, and conquers.

It is scarcely, I think, in human nature to combine two attitudes of mind, so apparently antipathetic; but Mr Mackenzie is always plausible, and the result attracts, by its ingenious originality. In the end we know not whether his heroine should be admired or scorned.

There remains " Guy and Pauline," which deals with persons we meet in the group already described, yet stands entirely outside it. Here Mr Mackenzie indulges his gift for romance without restraint, and may be described as idyllic. Self-analysis indeed remains, but the copious gift of ornamental language, elsewhere employed to startle, is here used for poetical effects; action or movement, elsewhere swift and abundant, are altogether omitted, and Bohemia turns pastoral. There are no naughty words or nasty ideas; no melodrama.

It is, in fact, one exquisitely prolonged love-scene, wherein, though curiously enough we have little sympathy with the chief actor, we are completely captured by the charm of the narrative. After the crowded sociability of intellectual Oxford, Guy had buried himself in the country to become a poet. It was no part of his ambition to write verse, and the experiment was, in fact, entirely unproductive. Almost immediately he is captivated by the vicar's daughter. Pauline is a dream girl, sweet and simple as when the world was young. Religious by training and instinct, warmly home-loving, and gaily affectionate, she is easily captured to naïve admiration of the lazy fluency and would-be subtlety in scepticism which make the Oxford manner.

Both are in love with love, thronging with exquisite fancies, blissfully happy to look and talk. It is only gradually, by slow degrees, after chapters of this dainty imagining, that we come to realise the shadow hovering in the background. For her part, Pauline is troubled in conscience by her lover's attitude towards religion, and the loosening of home ties involved by complete surrender. Guy has no money, no prospects, a practical, unsympathetic father, and a disastrous tendency to drift. What is scarcely even a formal engagement, with a perpetually deferred talk of marriage, finally murders hope. Pauline, facing his incapacity to bestow real happiness, closes the episode with fine moral courage. They part for ever.

It is impossible, I think, to express or convey the charms of this tale, with its monotony, its entire lack of drama, and its weak willed hero. The tragedy, which for her, at least, is final, seems merely perverse. But Mr Mackenzie has, nevertheless, achieved a double success. He has created two individual personalities (the woman's very exceptional and most attractive); he has written, intimately and at great length, of youth in the full tide of its first great discovery—the meaning of love. He is sincere and revealing, yet restrained, direct yet poetical, and everywhere without offence. There is absorbing emotion and intense joy, but no passion : rapturous phrasing, but no false note.

For the rest, Mr Mackenzie has tried various experiments, all with easy success. " Poor

Relations," for example, is pure comedy, vigorously handled, shrewdly observed, and very well calculated to afford us wholesome delight: an admirable piece of work.

We are content, with Mr Mais, to regard " The Passionate Elopement " as " simply a magnificent *tour de force*, an exquisite essay in literary bravura; a piece of loveliness thrown off by the artist as a young man while he was feeling his way," or, as Mr W. L. George expresses it more briefly, " a tale of powder and patches." Here, in fact, Mr Mackenzie plays with unvarnished romance: telling the old tale of a spoilt, foolish beauty and her wicked lover; of " drums, routs, auctions, ridottos, and masquerades; of drunken frolics, cock-baiting, and duelling "; pistols and postchaises, ruled by the beau of a Spa.

In " Rich Relatives " Mr Compton Mackenzie returns to the frankly romantic, introducing us, indeed, to Curtain Wells once more. It is a joyous, altogether delightful comedy, where the Italian-bred Jasmine, finding herself sadly orphaned, is driven to pass several depressing years in a series of visits to her rich uncles and aunts. Each family group presents its own eccentricities, contrasted dramatically, but rather prolonged as a continuous narrative; all are selfish and exacting, eager to make the young girl feel her dependence. There is a farcical touch, just sufficiently restrained to avoid jar, in Mr Harry Vibart's sudden, and most inopportune, appearances, which are, on every occasion, the cause of Jasmine's hurried banishment from wherever she showed signs of even beginning to feel at home.

Nevertheless, the devoted Harry, with the aid of a fairy-godmother great-uncle, finally effects Jasmine's release, and we leave her with a smile on her lips and joy in her heart.

Mr Mackenzie proves himself here to be the possessor of a pretty humour, most justly exercised upon the petty tyrannies of prosperous respectability, that would deny all freedom in thought or action, to the poor at its gates.

But there is one outstanding " figure of fun " in this merry tale, whose colossal absurdities approach genius. The great-uncle's dear old housekeeper, Selina, " belonged to one of those small sects " whose members are all firmly convinced of their own salvation, and contented to " damn the rest." Being, however, a kind-hearted soul, it needs the stimulus of righteous wrath to maintain her orthodoxy :

> " There have been times when I've wondered if the Lord was a little bit too particular. You know what I mean, a little too dictatorial and old-fashioned. But I give you my word since I've had two months of them I sympathise with Him. Yes, I sympathise with Him. And if I was Him, I'd do the same thing. Well, I never expected to enjoy looking down out of heaven at a lot of poor souls burning, but if this goes on much longer I shall begin to think that it's one of the glories of Paradise."

Every word of Selina's—her naïve curiosity about whom she is likely to meet in the next world, her familiarity with God's will, her interview with her dead friend, and her shrewd comments upon the living—are a perpetual delight. We are deeply grateful to Mr Mackenzie for his Selina.

"Carnival," on the other hand, has more in common with the Sinister series, Jenny, the Islington columbine, having a certain kinship to Sylvia Scarlett. She is a Cockney dream-heroine—"lazy, laughing, languid Jenny"—set in a similar background of the Charing Cross Road. Original, too, in her instincts, common only to her unstable lover, ultimately found wanting.

It is, nevertheless, the Sinister group which challenges judgment, by which I imagine Mr Mackenzie would elect to stand. They were criticised, on their first appearance, for their excess of freedom in language and subject, and here, certainly, he follows the error of realism by almost limiting truth to a record of sin. But there is a youthful exuberance and gaiety in his defiance of the conventions which disarms rebuke; a rapid brilliance in narrative, and rich colouring in atmosphere, which redeems the gloom and illumines the melodrama.

Mr Mackenzie is among the realists, but not actually one of them. He is curious about life, excited by it, and must be talking of his discoveries and adventures; wherein we find his own vitality and imagination not deadened by contact, but stirred rather to ever more daring activity. He is so keen to explore, so alert to observe, so quick to assimilate, that he is neither entangled, submerged, nor embittered by actual truth. Life seems to offer him a crowded playground, where the wonderful children of his imagination can be for ever exhibiting new pranks for our delight. His moving pictures are full of elaborate detail, and the full-blooded persons of the drama betray their modernity by fairly frequent worry about the Universe and their own souls, thereby bringing him in line with contemporary fiction. But his art derives most from his own eager curiosity, his young joy in life, and the vigorous personality of his characters. Owing comparatively little to exact observation, stirred by instinct, imagination, and taste, seeking only to entertain, he is innocent of moral intention, with no lesson to enforce, no philosophy to maintain.

In his "apology" at the end of "Sinister Street," Mr Mackenzie complains that many critics have persisted in regarding the book merely "as an achievement of memory," and treating it as an idealised or debased presentation of his own existence up to the age of twenty-three. Admittedly, however, he chose his own public school and his own college at Oxford, not recognising the right of schoolmasters to be exempt from the privilege of public men to be sometimes caricatured, but not attempting a single portrait of a don.

Whether or not this story of a youth, "who presumably will be a priest," was worth writing at such length depends finally, he claims, upon the number of people who can bear to read about it. "A work of art is bounded by the capacity of the spectator to apprehend it as a whole."

THE PASSIONATE ELOPEMENT	1911
CARNIVAL	1912
SINISTER STREET, I	1913
SINISTER STREET, II	1914
GUY AND PAULINE	1915
SYLVIA SCARLETT	1918
SYLVIA AND MICHAEL	1919
POOR RELATIONS	1919
THE VANITY GIRL	1920
RICH RELATIONS	1921

J. C. SNAITH

Mr Snaith, almost alone among his contemporaries, is an incurable romantic, frankly indifferent to the demands of realism.

It is not, even, only in atmosphere and incident that he depends on imagination and the fanciful. His characters, though human, stand outside humanity.

The distinction is most striking in " William Jordan, Junior," the story of a poet of " universal power given to no other person in the modern or the ancient world," the " divine simplicity " of whose " mighty cadences, which swept the whole gamut of the emotions," was such that the " humblest street persons who walked the street of the great city would be able to cherish them for their truth." " Why salute you him whom none honour? " asked the aged man of one who came all the way from Aberdeen to look upon the poet. " I am afraid, sir," answered the Northerner, " it must be left to my great-great-grandchildren to answer your question." He had, indeed, written for posterity.

Mr Snaith has portrayed William Jordan with loving care. Born and nurtured in the " little room" behind a dingy second-hand book-shop, he is a true dream-child. Guessing at no ambition beyond the acquirement of knowledge from dusty folios, drinking in eagerly the wisdom of the ancients, worshipping the Olympians, his tongue learns a strange language, his brain harbours strange thoughts. There is in him infinite dread and humility towards common men; infinite confidence in the rewards of industry: "*Of course, when I have learnt it all, I shall commence author.*"

Tenderly sheltered through childhood by a loving father no less sublimely indifferent than he to the world of affairs, William is driven at last into life by the shadow of poverty, threatening banishment from the "little room." Once personally confronted by "street persons," he realises that to enlighten mankind he must know man, and after a studious, wondering examination of the unmusical language and trivial ideas filling the newspapers, he adventures forth trembling, and yet determined. "That boy, beloved one," said his father on their first journey, "maintains his place in the scheme by removing the mud from the boots of the passers-by." Later, having discovered, by observation and deduction, the need for having his hair cut, William junior congratulated himself on the "self-contained manner in which he had given the hairdresser street-person a large piece of silver for his great kindness and courtesy."

He had determined, indeed, that this great

problem of living in the world must be undertaken without parental help or guidance, and, despite his incredible naïveté, actually obtains a post in a publisher's.

Drama, at this point, intervenes from daily association and an extraordinary sort of friendship with a slightly older youth, who combines knowing vulgarity with an unreasoning instinct for poetical nobility, which puzzles no one more than himself. He introduces young William to some of his gay friends, and to the theatre, whence that dazzled philosopher concludes that, after all, these " millions of street persons "— in their bright dresses and jewels—" were the true Olympians."

Also he finds that " the need of obtaining pieces of silver had grown as great as that of drawing the breath of life." Unfortunately, however, he had received no information as to the rights of property, and having particular occasion for the said " pieces of silver," calmly and innocently appropriates " just the very number required " from his employer's table, and, on learning that the loss has seriously worried the good gentleman, quietly explains what he had done—and why. The consequences prove sadly puzzling to one so thoroughly clear about the goodness of his intentions; but he accepts imprisonment without a murmur, chiefly concerned, it would seem, to study this new phase of life and understand the attitude of his accusers.

Naturally, the disgrace closes every avenue of employment to one in himself so ill-equipped for the battle of life, but by the indulgence of his old father, and the unwavering loyalty of his friend, William is enabled and induced to devote the remainder of his short existence to the pursuit of immortality. He blinds himself by incessant toil, poor nourishment, and lack of air or exercise; lives to dictate the whole poem, to hear of its publication and handle the precious volume, listen to kindly invented applause from a public, which had, in fact, proved cold and indifferent.

Here the character is pure fantasy, the circumstances frankly impossible, but Mr Snaith never loses control, never yields to strain. The poet, for all his detachment from humanity, is pre-eminently lovable, genuinely simple-minded, bent on a clearly-defined ideal. There is just that slight difference, most nicely balanced, between him and his old father, which would be produced by the old man's wider experience (mainly acquired through marriage) and more varied circumstances. On the other hand, the very imp of normal modernity fits perfectly into the picture. He is " bothered " by young Jordan, the visionary, impatient with himself for loving the lad, serving and cherishing him, but powerless against the spell. Average humanity, after all, responds to the highest appeal, recognises pure goodness, and is ready for sacrifice after worship.

These people, and these things, could not be. Yet if they were, this is just how they would be. The " romance " is true.

J. C. SNAITH

Mr Snaith's " Sailor," " with all the oceans of the world in his face," reveals no less Romance, by methods opposed to these in almost every particular. Henry Harper goes through, not less, but far more melodramatic experience than falls to the lot of average mankind. He is no less a dreamer than young Jordan, equally pledged to quixoticism, but also a man of his fists, inured to the trouble of life, blessed, or cursed, by genius as a novelist, which wins immediate popular recognition. Nursed by cruel blows and fiendish tyranny, entering the world among brutal seamen, educating himself o' nights while a champion at football, rubbing shoulders with all the villains and vulgarians of a busy world, he blunders at last into the very heart of that queer partnership between a theatrical underworld and cultured (literary and artistic) refinement, which is the favourite hunting ground of to-day's novelists. Sticking doggedly to his original conception of an ideal, combining the " Man of the World," and the " English Gentleman," he finds himself caught in the toils by the " eternal triangle," but in the light of his own purity achieves honour and happiness.

Personality here dominates, not by sheer innocence, but by straight, clean vigour. He does not, like Jordan, stand away from life, but, plunging head foremost into the vortex, beats the devil by his impetuous right hand. Haunted with the perverse ideal to be as others, without sacrifice to conscience, he actually succeeds in the heroic attempt.

He is romantic by excess, positively not negatively. He does not analyse himself or others, does not search for experience, theorise from observation, or worry about his soul. Taking life and men as he finds them, facing the hard knocks, grateful for joy and sunshine, he just fights along over his private battlefield, trusting his own crude, wholely instinctive, notions of right and wrong. He is a knight of the Middle Ages, set right in the midst of the very latest moral and social complexities of civilisation. And the " genie within that elemental soul never slept."

Nevertheless, as in " William Jordan, Junior," Mr Snaith writes with all that glow of romance which ignores the minutiæ of the actual. The chosen character, framed on abstract heroism, is painted without shadow, clear cut, rigidly outlined, quite impossibly consistent: more true to type than nature.

Once more, too, Mr Snaith convinces us that his method is deliberate, selected by taste, not imposed by the limitations of his own power; since much of the atmosphere, many of the minor dramatis personæ, are very triumphs of realism. The noble Klondyke, " firmly convinced that with the rudiments of reading and writing, and a straight left with a punch in it, you could go all over the world," may be dismissed, indeed, as a figure of romance; but the immortal Ginger (" a great believer in depth," loyal and true to Harper); that charming female (who " understood that no unmarried lady could read

Thackeray and remain respectable "); the bookseller and Tim in the bookshop; those " old ladies of fearless and terrific virtue " (who gave the " glad eye " to Henry Harper); the genial Editor; Cora, the fair and frail (who, tempting him to " compromise " her, forces Henry into a wretched marriage) : even the heroine, Mary (because she hesitates about her man), do not any one of them quite escape the half-tones of modernity. They are observed with fine subtlety, painted with surface values.

No less modern in atmosphere and local colour, but on the other hand wholly innocent of realism, come " Araminta " and " Love Lane," in which Mr Snaith subdues the older conventionally constructed fiction to the romance spirit. There is, indeed, a certain charming, inconsequent absurdity about " the Goose " (who is Araminta), which is unique. She has really no right to her delightful drawl, but, as a Gainsborough reincarnate, naturally captivates society, just because she finds everyone " such a sweet." Mr Snaith plays very neatly with the two middle-aged, cynical peers of the realm, her rival wooers; the dragon aunt who adopts and exhibits her; the sentimental companion " with a romantic tale on her eyelashes "; the handsome young artist hero; and her sister, Muffin.

That, having secured her promise—since he can help papa, brothers, and sisters—Lord Cheriton should, most magnanimously, hand her over to the lover who had, for his part, renounced all claim, provides an unexpected dénouement, lending just that touch of unreality and pretty sentiment needed to harmonise the picture. In such tales the heroine may weep, but she must not despair. Grief, that were prolonged or final, would be out of place.

"Love Lane" strikes rather a deeper note, mainly through its war colouring. We have the familiar, prosperous, and pig-headed father who bullies his wife and children. One daughter leaves home as a militant suffragette, and her "Joan of Arc profile overlaid by a general air of you-be-damnedness made an ideal picture postcard." Another is cast off because she marries a ne'er-do-well. It is, however, her husband who, as one easily foresees from the first, proves to be the hero. He is regenerated by the war, which "took anything superfluous in the way of talk out of him, as it did with most." Mr Snaith accepts, without question, the more sentimental view of a war that "equalised men," while the "British Empire rose at once to a moral height without a precedent in the history of the world" —which is, of course, one side of the truth. Under such influences, William Hollis—greengrocer—enjoys a second honeymoon (his forty-eight hours leave) with the faded woman, his wife, which—for all its flavour of the Sunday School, is drawn with restrained sympathy, perfectly true to human nature.

Inevitably the old man repents, and in the intervals of managing his native town as few towns were managed in those difficult days, helps his forgiven daughter, and honours the sergeant, his feckless son-in-law, who "died that his faith and his friends might live."

There is, admittedly, nothing very original or striking in the story, but Mr Snaith's instinct for simplicity is sure and sound, and one respects a conventionality so sincere.

Moreover, in books like "Mary Plantagenet," "Mrs Fitz," "Fortune," "Lady Barbarity," and "The Great Age," Mr Snaith gaily accepts other conventions with similarly charming results. These are all tales without anxiety, frankly made to type, but thoroughly bright and stirring. Fitz, for example, is an Anthony Hope hero in an Anthony Hope situation. Morganatically married to the "Crown Princess of Allyria," he embarks (with all the naïvety of melodrama) upon the most perilous adventures to hold her he has won, dragging a few conventional Britishers at his heels, reluctant indeed, but sportsmen to the core. The preposterous Englishman in "Fortune" is the same type, flourishing in an earlier century, and more purely quixotic in aim. His methods and nature are, inevitably, far more crude, but he, too, achieves the impossible by bluff. One cannot wonder at the proud young Spaniard who had heard of the English as "a dreadful, brawling people, a race of robbers, who sold their swords for gain, and overran the whole of Europe," whereas "now I know the world better, I have learnt that all Englishmen are mad."

When Lady Barbarity cries, "I blushed divinely, I knew I did. I was seated opposite a mirror (which I generally am)," we recognise the type at once. This eighteenth century beauty " will not wed a clothes-pole, will not wed a snuff-box "—she wants " a man." And " when I die let it be done to slow music, and I mean to have a funeral in the Abbey if I can." You know she will lose her heart to a handsome rebel, dress him up in girls' clothes, and dance through the pages in a gay duel with the stern, but not entirely black-hearted, officer of the King. Pranks these, sullying the most tenacious honour of that " poor vamped-up old gentleman," her papa, otherwise a cynical reprobate. You know too, she will get her way and marry the brave boy.

In his latest volume, " The Council of Seven," Mr Snaith " steps out with a rattling good thriller." This brisk tale of mystery is distinguished by its fine writing.

" Mary Plantagenet " rules her world (the present) no less divinely, but her manners are more sedate; though she grew up in a policeman's family and became a queen of the stage. Fortunately, however (in the last chapter), she proves to be the (legitimate) daughter of an old nobleman and his maid-servant, so that no permanent obstacle survives to her marriage with the well-born hero. There is, however, considerable subtlety in the drawing of Mary's mother, who combines real strength and independence of character, with the most deeply ingrained ideal of deference to her " betters "—almost a passionate conviction of *reality* in class differences. The instinct produces, in the main, quiet comedy, but is quite seriously meant, and, if touched with exaggeration, yet rings sincere.

Mr Snaith's next novel, "The Adventurous Lady," falls in the group of pure romance in a modern setting, some of the minor characters being drawn with a certain degree of realism. The plot is based on the mad scheme of an imperious beauty, Lady Elfrida, who forces the modest little governess, Girlie Cass, to take her place on a visit to a certain family of wealth, and not quite assured position, who have arranged a charitable performance in which she was to play the heroine. The well-born one resented this, because her parents expected her to "catch" a rich parti, who, being newly titled, did not quite suit her ladyship's idea of a husband. Also she welcomes the adventure of posing as a meek instructor of youth; though, when it comes to the point, she is at small pains to sustain the rôle. Neither lady, in fact, really plays up to her assumed part, but each remains, charmingly, herself.

Complications, of course, arise, which, if temporarily trying to those concerned, are not to be taken seriously, and, in effect, each of the young girls secures thereby a most satisfactory husband who, under normal conditions, could not have even ever seen her.

This is all very trivial matter, touched with a light hand. But, as ever, Mr Snaith reveals more subtlety than one would expect. The twin heroines have each decided personality, very delicately revealed. Each lover is a Man, though two more different persons it would be almost impossible to imagine.

The minor characters, and the events, are drawn with humorous vigour : none of them commonplace or obvious.

" The Great Age " (Elizabeth's), indeed, would almost dispose one to declare that, after all, Mr Snaith's chief attribute must be his courage—a total indifference to the critic. The structure of its plot is identical with that of " Lady Barbarity "; its " leading gentleman," that " illiterate merry-andrew," Will Shakespeare. Nor do the manifold perils of such a course seem to daunt him one whit. Sweet Anne's treasonable heroism has precisely the same consequences for her loyal parent : she is equally determined to marry the rescued prisoner. As to William Shakespeare, we are shown his thoughts, we hear his words—with as great a freedom as if he were purely a creature of the imagination. Here, perhaps, Mr Snaith is wise. Had he paused to consider how much, or how little, he dare say, the problem could only have enjoined silence. Mainly, I think, from " Hamlet "; partly, no doubt, from such biographical fragments as we possess; he has conceived the man : and *then* given full reins to his own imagination. Being himself full of romance, attracted by chivalrous heroism, and a " spacious " humanity that is at once tender and whimsical, he does not, in the main, affront taste. We are content with his Shakespeare. It suggests much; does no violence to our ideal. His intimate familiarity with every drama and character lights up the incidents of the adventure, colours his language throughout. It is most satisfying of all in the rare wit of one brief word-duel between dramatist and tragedian, Master Shakespeare and his friend Burbage.

In detail, occasionally, Mr Snaith's easy fluency has led him somewhat astray. There are paragraphs repeated almost word for word, a few rather shameless anachronisms in phrasing, and a definite confusion as to just when, and just why, Shakespeare fixed upon Anne to play Rosalind. *Twice* we read, the idea came *first* into his mind.

We gladly accept, however, the whole story as, like its comrades from the same pen, a pure romance. The presence of Queen Elizabeth and her court, of Shakespeare and his friends, gives it a certain permanence they lack; but in all this group, even more than in the longer novels of modern life, Mr Snaith has no concern with exactitude, analysis, observation, or realism in any form. He gives us merely a charming tale and delightful characters, with efficient craft. The diet is singularly refreshing.

There are finally several reasons for considering Mr Snaith's first novel, " Broke of Covenden," as a work apart. Because it falls more nearly in line with the contemporary manner, modern critics have often regretted that the author never quite maintained his early promise.

Squire Broke, indeed, is an old-fashioned character. " That money was the end and the beginning, the beginning and the end was to his mediaeval mind as fantastic as to suppose that a tradesman could be a gentleman." His wife has a far finer intellect, yet she knew that " the instant she set up her own indomitable will against his she must be overthrown . . . the man's inalienable prerogative still remained to him of knocking her down." His friend, too, recognised " the excellent matrimonial principle of giving his wife clothes in exchange for her cookery," and Uncle Charles, who " was *not* one of the haw-haw brigade," declared of the squire's daughters that " these little fillies are like that bow-legged bull-bitch of mine—a damn sight too full of breed. . . . I always say a woman's the same as a good bitch, the breed makes all the difference. She may strike you as ugly at first, but just wait until you've gone over her points, and you'll find out she's about as handsome as paint."

Into this atmosphere of stark prejudice and unyielding traditionalism, Mr Snaith introduces many essentially modern types: the new rich; Lord Salmon who entertains spaciously and " seems hardly to know whom to admire most—himself or the radiant persons he saw around him "; the poor, clever bookseller's son, who, after leaving the University, " had to lose the habit of looking at life with an eyeglass."

The whole story, indeed, naturally develops into a bitter struggle between the old and the new; one of the most favourite topics among Mr Snaith's contemporaries. It is revealed, moreover, with that careful understanding of both sides, that scrupulous search after first causes, which is the essence of modernity. Fiction to-day has concerned itself with many a " hard-shell " parent, no less inhumanly consistent than Broke himself, no less diabolical in obstinate cruelty. The nimbler wits and the cynical tolerance of the " nursery party " may confound, but cannot shake them. The Squire meets with two rebels in his own family to whom he is adamant in cruelty; and the " middle way " of Mrs Broke towards them, reveals a keen power in the author for emotional analysis and minute observation. Indeed, her heart, her intellect, and her actions almost produce three separate and independent entities, as is often the way with the moderns. Hovering, too, over the whole narrative, we recognise that sense of fatalism which haunts the sceptic, that conception of powerlessness in the individual against the tyranny of life, which governs so much thought to-day.

Mr Snaith does not grant victory either to Broke or his children: it may be said that all suffer alike, even though Delia marries happily in the end; conquest for her comes through much bitterness and a great hardening of the heart. Truce between the generations is, indeed, proved impossible, and the perversity of circumstances makes the worst of a bad job. There are broken hearts, lingering deaths, crushed hopes among the family, and to the rest, nothing much left worth living for.

Perhaps in one respect "Broke of Covenden" may be placed first in the list—for its greater diversity of persons, all delineated with wit and mastery. It is an admirably artistic piece of work, instinct with drama, and an absorbing story—both for characterisation and event. But it might, I think, have been written (save for its incidental phrasing) by several of Mr Snaith's contemporaries, with no less enjoyment: whereas "The Sailor" and "William Jordan" are quite original and unique.

These stand, with his other "romances," for a class of fiction which, though contrary to the currents prevailing to-day, has been thereby proved, not only still vital and vigorous, but quite at home in the atmosphere and surroundings of modern life, equally adapted to the revelation of old world, or up-to-date, types of character.

The fact is, Mr Snaith has a firm hand. The strenuous moderns, no doubt, will criticise his subject matter, but they dare not despise the treatment. Realism may embrace life: Mr Snaith has taught us it cannot appropriate human nature.

BROKE OF COVENDEN	1904
HENRY NORTHCOTE	1906
WILLIAM JORDAN, JUNIOR	1907
ARAMINTA	1909
FORTUNE	1910
MRS FITZ	1910
LADY BARBARITY	
THE PRINCIPAL GIRL	1912
AN AFFAIR OF STATE	1914
THE GREAT AGE	1915

J. C. SNAITH

THE SAILOR	1916
LOVE LANE	1918
MARY PLANTAGENET	1918
THE ADVENTUROUS LADY	1921
THE COUNCIL OF SEVEN	1922

E. M. FORSTER

THERE is something elusive about Mr Forster which sets him apart from his contemporaries, lending a certain quiet distinction to his work. He certainly does not imitate Henry James, yet there is much—particularly in " Howard's End "—that carries us back to that past master of reticences. We feel all the old reserve of power, the turn of phrase that dominates while it puzzles, the insight that penetrates without exposure, the smooth quiet suddenly breaking out into dramatic violence. Unlike the extreme realist, Henry James and Mr Forster reveal the depths without lifting the veil. They do not undress their characters or obtrude their souls; here are no cuts or screams, no staring scars left by the surgeon's knife. They are not obviously bursting with self-expression: crawling among the passions, " to see the wheels go round "; solemn vivisectors of Man.

Yet they know more, and unfold more, of mind and the emotions. Theirs are no vague platitudes of protest, but an assured vision. The strenuous self-analyst may, and frequently does, disturb our most cherished convictions. To provoke thought, to disturb complacency, is stimulating to the mind. It provides, as it were, a good start.

But inspiration—the will to good—derives from fact, not fumbling; from conclusions, not from investigators. The writer who may seem, perhaps, less at pains to " speak truth and shame the devil," will often reach far more deeply into the mainspring of human nature, and give us far more of the truth : simply because he has been through all the other is struggling so conscientiously to express, assimilated his experience, and applied it to his creative art.

We may admit, indeed, that the subject matter of " Where Angels Fear to Tread " might have been chosen by any one of Mr Forster's immediate contemporaries. We have the conventions, represented by a family diverse in individual temperament, but strongly knit together by the most determined amour-propre. A daughter of the house marries unwisely—an impossible Italian, boyish, uncouth, somewhat primitive and mercenary, quite irresponsible, strongly disposed to change. After the first fine glow of happiness following rebellion, she dies— more or less in misery; and, at their mother's bidding, the " superior " brother, a crudely religious sister, and a friend, rashly embark on a mission to rescue her baby son.

No sensible person would have foreseen difficulties; the material gain is so obvious, the grandmother's love so natural. Only foreigners, alas, are so different ! It is quite incomprehensible : the father loves his child, and the play begins.

There is, at first, slow movement, subtle digression, much interplay—charming to watch —between English and Latin, common-sense and romance. We attend a concert, admire the scenery, study the ways of Italian peasantry. Money is offered, terms discussed. Trembling, but not yet moved to the depths, we alternate between success and failure, hope and despair. The widower proves sublime as parent, yet only half a man : charming indeed, thoroughly a good fellow, but practically quite perverse.

Then suddenly, without a note of warning, things begin to happen. Once set in motion, they rush. Strong in her faith, sister Harriet steals the infant; hurrying with it secretly to the station, lets the poor child fall and die. In her own eyes henceforth for ever a murderer, reason loses its sway. Not unnaturally, Gino (widower) strives to murder Philip (brother), and, as a last flash of unreason, the friend, Miss Abbott, most staid, most conventional of mortals, declares she was all the time " worshipping every inch of him, and every word he spoke," while " all through he had taken her for a superior being."

To Philip " she seemed to be transfigured, and to have, indeed, no part with refinement or unrefinement any longer." There was no more to be said or done because " all the wonderful things had happened."

In " The Longest Journey " Mr Forster has given us a rather more obvious, and continuous, struggle between the vision and what he calls "the teacup of experience—oh! that teacup! To be taken at prayers, at friendship, at love, till we are quite sane, quite experienced, and quite useless to God or man."

This, then, is the fruit of life for Mr Pembroke—schoolmaster, in whose presence all "conversation became pure and colourless and full of under-statements"; while, "just as if he were a real clergyman, neither men nor boys ever forgot that he was there."

Unfortunately, Rickie, the dreamer, fully imagined himself in love with Agnes, sister to this paragon, who "caught him, and makes him believe that he caught her. That's what I mean when I say that she is a lady"—as a cynical undergraduate friend expressed it. Both Pembrokes had the same tiresome habit of "taking life with a laugh—as if life were a pill."

Needless to say, marriage between these irreconcilables produces friction. Everything turns upon Rickie's half-brother, Stephen, the illegitimate offspring, *not*, as he had always believed, of his smilingly selfish father, but of the mother he worshipped.

Stephen is a strange, wild creature, frequently drunk, always uncouth and bitter, yet a man. The Pembrokes, driven to action, finally repudiate the "impossible" creature, treating him with a refined cruelty and torture, which exasperates Rickie to revolt. Wherefore the lame, sensitive youth—driven to exile—rescues the drunken Stephen at a level crossing, sacrificing his own life in the act.

We leave Mr Pembroke " arranging " the hero's " Literary Remains " for publication, Agnes married again to a pre-eminently " suitable " nonentity, Stephen wholly absorbed in his own child—not precisely a reformed character, but very clearly inspired by moral purpose.

Here are, as we said, more continuous dramatic happenings, a more complex plot, a more normal—and more crowded—story. There are characters of marked individuality, and great interest, not even named in the above summary; people with theories, tragedies, and eccentricities of their own. There is a vivid picture of undergraduate life and talk, an " original," strong-minded aunt, a few schoolboys, and others, to fill the canvas.

We note, too, that, unlike his contemporaries, Mr Forster would not exalt the metropolis: " There's no such thing as a Londoner. He's only a country man on the road to sterility." We are, again, almost persuaded to accept the distinction, and preference, of Rickie's uncle for " coarseness revealing something," as opposed to " vulgarity concealing something."

Still, even here, Mr Forster writes deliberately, with firm reticence, and a subtle humour, that hints at far more than is ever actually said.

It is, however, in " Howard's End " that our author recalls, most definitely, Henry James;

partly, perhaps, because the spiritual significance here rests on the mystic influence of a charming house, the " atmosphere " of bricks and mortar, as it was, once at least, used by the master. This is, in many ways, Mr Forster's most subtle, most finished, and most successful novel. The under-currents are so deep; the emotions, not more than half understood by those who experience them, are so sensitive, that the whole thing might very easily be dismissed as much ado about nothing. Such a view would, of course, be quite superficial, as Mr Forster has found occasion to reveal characters as fascinating as they are rare.

The deep-lying contrast between Margaret and her sister is vivid and fundamental by very reason of its being always implied rather than stated. The baffling pathos of Mrs Wilcox is as subtle and thought provoking as any portrait in fiction. Her children's real natures are almost hidden under their vivid talk and emphasised surface emotions. Then we have Leonard and his private tragedy, almost, but not quite, an independent novel in miniature. Finally, the romance of Margaret; the strange fate which ends in marriage with her best friend's husband, and brings her to " Howard's End," after all.

Few writers, I think, could have reconciled us to such a dénouement. There had been so much, only the more real for its lack of strain or morbidity, between her and the first Mrs Wilcox, that it would seem perilously near sacrilege to have replaced her. Yet we accept it without criticism.

Margaret moves through these pages, puzzling, hesitating, maybe, not always sure of her own mind, even her own desire; yet a complete woman, slowly but surely developing towards what she was bound, from the first, to become. Generous to a fault, always keen, sympathetic, and quick to help others, she is yet, at bottom, sure of herself, never permanently in doubt between essentials and trivialities, knowing what to seek, how to receive.

Here, again, we notice the same device in construction which appeared in " The Longest Journey "; a quiet, subdued movement, marshalling men and events into their seemingly obscure relations, until the end slips out with a rush, crises tumble over each other's heels, and we awake to " what good came of it at last." We see, then, all was inevitable, convincing, and true to life.

Mr Forster has also written that strange group of tales called " The Celestial Omnibus," on which, to many readers, his chief claim to serious consideration must be allowed to rest. Personally, I do not accept this judgment. Possibly from prejudice against the supernatural in fiction; not from any devotion to realism, only because it weakens the glamour of true romance.

Here, for the most part, we read of " Fawns in Wiltshire "; those " who have been in the woods and understand things "; the tree-woman who " will never forget her earth-lover, never, as long as she has branches to shade men from the sun "; the " Road from Colonus " where " a supreme event would transfigure the face of the world." But in " The Celestial Omnibus " and " The Other Side of the Hedge " he attempts, of course allegorically, certain mystic revelations of Heaven, or the Hereafter. The " Omnibus " carries its passengers among the Heroes of Past Days—gods, philosophers, and captains of men. Admission is granted only to him who can " Stand by Himself. . . . For poetry is a spirit, and they that would worship it must worship in spirit and in truth." Leaving the Road of Life, passing through " the Hedge," a pilgrim looks on " some who were singing, some talking, some engaged in gardening, haymaking, or other rudimentary industries. They all seemed happy, and I might have been happy too, if I could have forgotten that the place led nowhere." In this land many material " things did not work." It all meant " nothing but itself." Wherefore, because " mankind have other aims," the pilgrim turns back to the Road.

What is required of us that we sense these things? What quality can we detect in the curate who saw the Fawn, the boy who heard the Call, the girl who " escaped absolutely " to the " other kingdom "? It is something " for which truthfulness is too cold a name, and animal spirits too coarse a one."

They are, indeed, rare souls to whom Mr Forster has lent much charm, but we miss, somehow, the heart of them, nor can we read their message—at least for man. Yet in fiction, maybe, they have a place: carrying us into the mists and meanings of Mother Earth, speaking with the tongues of angels, hovering like fair spirits of light over the grime and weariness of material realities.

Every way, as we have shown, Mr Forster stands apart. Whether he has written so seldom because he has not over much to say, or from some excellent standard of art in his own mind, these few volumes are a great gift. They are distinguished, without blur or hesitancy, really original, and reveal great power in characterisation and the reading of all within a man. Theirs is the soul-romance, born of love for nature and things spiritual; miles away from melodrama and adventure, quite without vain imaginings of perfectability.

WHERE ANGELS FEAR TO TREAD
THE LONGEST JOURNEY
A ROOM WITH A VIEW
HOWARD'S END
THE CELESTIAL OMNIBUS

JOHN BUCHAN

Mr John Buchan I accept gratefully as a sign of the times, a sound type of competent efficiency. He has, of course, been many things besides a novelist, all of them with conspicuous, if not supreme, success. As a novelist, he is a master of his craft. The man who does what he undertakes well, in an interesting fashion, represents one, at least, of the conspicuous influences of our generation.

What one may call the material of his novels and short stories is not modern: their manner does not follow the road dear to his more strenuous contemporaries. They would annoy the " highbrow "; they do not satisfy those who yearn for a stricken soul, or love to plunge into the glamour and grime of sin. They are " plain tales " of romance and adventure, with only atmosphere and furniture up to date. And Mr Buchan admits, too, that fondness for crisp and knowing generalisations which youth always affects.

One may conveniently, and quite justly, illustrate his work in fiction by the consideration of three complete novels and two collections of short tales.

There is not, perhaps, much to say—with profit—about "Prester John" save that it is a quite admirable yarn, packed with murderous intrigue, hair-breadth escapes, deeds of reckless daring and the glamour of strange folk. Its canny hero adventures into the far corners of the earth, learns the secrets of many a coloured fanatic, helps to build the Empire, and triumphs over the tricks of his most deadly foes. The villainous, and yet inspired, Prester John himself long dreams, and indeed nearly achieves, a mystical Return of the Savage—to something approaching World-Power. A man born to kingship, holding himself an ally of God, this black-hearted pagan was a sincere enthusiast, believing in the divinity of his mission, feeling "behind him all the armies of heaven." His "blood-thirsty savage" followers were actually "consecrated to the meek service of Christ." His was the vision of a new "Ethiopian Empire, so majestic that the white man everywhere would dread its name, so righteous that all men under it would live in ease and peace. . . . Ye, the old masters of the land, are now the servants of the oppressor. And yet the oppressors are few, and the fear of you is in their hearts. . . . What have ye gained from the alien?" save "a bastard civilisation which has sapped your manhood; a false religion which would rivet on you the chains of a slave."

All of which may not be very much like real life anywhere, yet is not altogether foreign to human nature : it serves to stir the imagination, to rest the mind. Besides which there is sound stuff in our good Mr David Crawfurd, who has wit enough to confound the mystic.

In " Greenmantle " Mr Buchan has chosen a different field of adventure, leading his hero a devil's dance over the by-ways of Armageddon. This is a spy story of the Great War, wherein a plain Englishman, carrying his life in his hands, strives to penetrate and circumvent one of those baffling intrigues of the wily Teuton, by which they were credited with having attached the fighters of Islam to their side : " some tremendous sacred sanction, some holy thing, some book or gospel or some new prophet from the desert, something which would cast over the whole ugly mechanism of German war the glamour of the old torrential raid which crumpled the Byzantine Empire and shook the walls of Vienna." Here is, indeed, another and a more venomous Holy War to be encountered, which would " let hell loose in those parts pretty soon."

This " forlorn hope," to the solution of which those in authority had practically no clue whatever, carries our Richard Hannay into strange places among wild men. It may not, perhaps, be said that he achieves any material success, but he does penetrate to the very heart of the great mystery; he does see, and learn, much of the lady Greenmantle, whose long-looked-for coming should summon the Eastern hordes and " madden the Moslem peasant with dreams of Paradise." He finds, indeed, but small reason to " quite believe in Islam becoming a back number."

Incidentally we learn from these absorbing pages to echo the judgment of Mr John S. Blenkiron—of the United States—that " you Britishers haven't any notion how wide awake your Intelligence Service is. I reckon it's easy the best of all the belligerents."

We shall not, probably, go far wrong if we accept, for all it attempts to reveal, the following account of the German mind :

> " It is only boldness that can baffle them. They are a most diligent people. They will think of all likely difficulties, but not of all possible ones. They have not much imagination. They are like steam engines which must keep to prepared tracks. There they will hunt any man down, but let him trek for open country and they will be at a loss. Therefore boldness, my friend; for ever boldness. Remember as a nation they wear spectacles, which means that they are always peering."

" The Thirty-Nine Steps " is a war novel also. Here, however, the adventures occur mainly in Scotland; partly in London and Bradgate, Kent. We have here German agents, mingling in high politics, murdering a Greek Premier, stealing State secrets, and, in the process, disclosing a very considerable ingenuity, tireless energy, and reckless indifference to human life. There are chapters that recall " Kidnapped "—with a difference : for our hero is driven to exert all those fascinating devices of the trek-expert who yet, after all, owes so much to his genius for good luck. Mr Buchan, of course, is quite at home in the Highlands, and uses his knowledge with great effect. It is once more Richard Hannay who plays many new parts, a veritable master of make-up, true sportsman, and man of mettle. This is, as the author admits frankly, just a " dime novel " or " shocker," a " romance where the incidents defy the probabilities and march just inside the borders of the possible." Like Mr Buchan himself, however, " I have long cherished an affection for that elementary type of tale," which is truly an " aid to cheerfulness." The work is thoroughly well done; humorously varied, crowded with thrills and shocks, just sufficiently spiced with dramatic coincidences that please and startle, without strain or offence.

I am personally disposed to rate one quality in Mr Buchan's achievements rather exceptionally high. He resists, always and everywhere, the temptations towards perfectability. He does not plague us with the " complete " hero. His adventurers, inevitably, record many a hard-won triumph, and often score off their adversaries at the eleventh hour; but they are not invariably a success, not always cool and courageous, not masters of every weapon or of all men. They miss a chance, miscalculate and misjudge, do not perform miracles. Just because they are human; therefore our very good friends.

It is inevitable, perhaps, that we should ask how much these two novels have gained from that " inside " information about the war which their author was no doubt, in a most favourable position to acquire. They, probably, gain much: though I should presume that each actual framework, or plot, is quite imaginary. "Greenmantle," in particular, reads more like a very ingenious hint—as it were—of what *might* have been happening behind the scenes, than like a dramatic adaptation of actual dangers afoot. Here, as in "The Thirty-Nine Steps," it is most probable that Mr Buchan has only used his knowledge for the colouring of the atmosphere, to perfect the realism in detail, which is essential to modern romance.

Yet just because he was able to do this, and has done it, these tales remain (what many of their contemporaries have no pretence to be) a passably true picture, and most suggestive record, of certain phases in human experience, during a period when life was, in an ugly sense, romantic, and when many experiences we had long grown accustomed to call impossible, might actually come upon any of us at any moment.

It might be naturally supposed from the above analysis that Mr Buchan's Short Stories would follow the same lines in a more concentrated form. But they do, in fact, introduce a new element which, for want of a better word, we must call "supernatural." This is, indeed, characteristic of his generation. As we grow material, we become superstitious. The loosening of orthodoxy as a governing force in life has been always accompanied by keen interest, if not faith, in the older forms of religion; and, particularly since the war, average man has grown credulous. The historical investigation of Christianity, too, has induced many to find in all forms of belief some message from the one God, at least from the Spiritual Force behind creation generally so called.

Mr Buchan has skilfully used these tendencies, or forms of faith, for atmosphere, both in " The Moon Endureth " and in " The Watcher by the Threshold." Each contains tales of men possessed by the devil, haunted by strange visions, in touch with mysteries behind the veil. He attempts, also, to analyse the mind of those scientists who go mad over the fourth dimension, or perish in the pursuit of some almost miraculous discovery, carrying their great secret with them to the silent grave. He gives new life to many an old legend of the countryside, casting the weird, powerful influence of " place "—the local superstition—over the normal man. His wise men become as children, in their morbid seeking after the unknown truth, set in an old wives' tale. He introduces us, for example, in " No Man's Land "—a gruesome tragedy, to " the history of the craziest survival the world has ever seen . . . fragments of old religions, primeval names of god and goddess . . . the key to a hundred puzzles." His hero visits " the folk," hears and sees the " unmentionable deeds in darkness " of the half-animal Picts, lingering among the scarts of the Muncraw.

He writes of men, feeling the call of Wild Waters, stealing away to the woods that they may celebrate strange pagan rites, playing the hero in the old border raids, driven from fame and power at the bidding of a boy's dream.

The men and women of these "twice-told" tales are all on the verge of mania, supernormal, obsessed by the tyranny of One Idea, which must disturb the mind's balance, putting them "beyond the pale." It is attractive material for fiction, wisely handled in miniature, food for thought, not without service to the student of humanity who loves the "lands behind the mist."

For "the moon," said St Francis, "signified the dominion of all strange things in earth and air, such as were beyond the comprehension of man's reason or the authority of his temporal will." Also "the back-world of Scotland is a wise place to travel in for those who believe it is not bounded strictly by kirk and market-place, and who have an ear for old songs and lost romances."

Mr Buchan has given us, then, two versions of modernity, neither of them elsewhere so prominent among contemporary novelists, presented with equal skill: action and vision in the most extreme forms of which man is capable, the will to do and the will to dream. These are the two chief elemental forces in human nature, most contradictory, leading to thoughts ever opposed, yet for ever the very stuff and fibre of our nature. From life we shall always demand both; each provides first-class matter for the real drama of romance.

Though not formally a collection of short

stories, his last novel, "The Path of the King," is actually a series of episodes with a new hero, or heroine, to each. They are all, however, members of one family; descended, more or less directly, from one Viking ancestor; and, having royal blood in their veins, are destined one day to achieve kingship. Mr Buchan contends, and ingeniously illustrates his contention, that " however heroism may lapse for more than a generation, it will emerge at the long last. It will not, most probably, appear in the direct line—among the first-born, from whom much comforting hath driven out the devil—but a younger son of younger sons will, in due course, rise from the gutter, and, by force of the character he has inherited from bygone centuries, become the man."

The theme affords ample opportunity for brisk drama and varied adventure. It carries us through many centuries into the far corners of the world. It provides costume and atmosphere, of many colours. Mr Buchan controls his motley crew with great craft and easy mastery. He recaptures the past, and gives us a well-drawn pocket History of the World.

It is all, as usual, very competent, very pleasing and sufficient unto itself. What he attempts, he achieves.

SIR QUIXOTE	1895
SCHOLAR GIPSIES	1896
JOHN BURNET OF BARNS	1898
GREY WEATHER	1899
A LOST LADY OF OLD YEARS	1899

HALF-HEARTED	1900
THE WATCHER BY THE THRESHOLD	1902
A LODGE IN THE WILDERNESS	1906
PRESTER JOHN	1910
THE MOON ENDURETH	1912
SALUTE TO ADVENTURERS	1915
GREENMANTLE	1916
MR STANDFAST	1919
THE THIRTY-NINE STEPS	1919
THE PATH OF THE KING	1921

NEIL LYONS

I HAVE deliberately included Mr Neil Lyons in this volume to ensure completeness in representing the period under review. The movement in fiction from romance to realism (itself historically continuous) has been always accompanied by the lowering of social status in the dramatis personæ. Though Samuel Richardson no doubt loved a lord, he wrote chiefly for, and about, the middle class, and his lead was accepted without demur. It is, of course, Charles Dickens whom we all associate most intimately with the " lower " orders, though they had, in fact, been occasionally presented, with far less sentimentality, in the eighteenth century. More recently, George Gissing penetrated, with savage bitterness, below the living wage; H. G. Wells and others have taken up the small shopkeeper and the clerk in the suburbs. Extreme realists, to-day, enter the Pub and the Lounge, the Night Club and the Promenade, the Green-Room and the Flat.

But whereas their search is for Sin, their aim defiance and exposure, there have been with us for some time now a group of writers in slum life who, though primarily seekers of copy or character-types, may be fairly described as the literary exponents of the " settlement " movement—which is a prominent phase of the time. Obvious examples were " No. 5 John Street," " Tales of Mean Streets," and Arthur Morrison's " To London Town."

Now of this group Mr Neil Lyons is at once the most copious, most sympathetically intimate, most frankly gay, and, by virtue of his delightful war-sketches from a Y.M.C.A. hut, most up-to-date. He is admittedly a journalist, casual in touch, hasty in judgment, rather too sure of himself, and addicted to infallibility. But, on the other hand, while not blind to tragedy or emotion, and not indifferent to either, he has been entirely successful in avoiding the Sunday School flavour of Mr Pett Ridge and other exponents of the " dear " poor.

Mr Neil Lyons, indeed, depends on his humour : which is not only keen and racy, but thoroughly well-in-hand, soundly constructed, and a perpetual delight. One should not, of course, read his work *en masse*, in an academic spirit of criticism, or as a study in social philosophy. Taken in small doses, it is a stimulating tonic, enlarging our sympathies with human nature, prompting to laughter and tears. He has both humour and wit, keenly developed, with a strong vein of hilarious originality, based on a rare gift for dialogue, skilled phonetics, and a dramatic sense.

In " Arthur's " Mr Lyons exploits the coffee-stall, always his favourite haunt, a veritable tramp's club. Hence life is seen at a peculiar angle, "during the hours when London sleeps; all save those for whom business or pleasure compel departure from the habits of mankind." If not conventionally select, the society at Arthur's is, after its own standard, exclusive. The genial proprietor has tests of his own for entry, his own summary methods of expulsion. He is a charitable soul, but particular. "I like that gal's face, she washes it," as he once remarked. The men and women of his circle are all genuine pals who, whatever the consequences, play the game. Always outspoken and ready enough with their fists, they are, in essentials, loyal and neighbourly—without vulgar inquisitiveness into each other's private affairs; merry and irresponsible on ordinary occasions, they prove capable, at a crisis, of real heroism and self-sacrifice. They have a pretty wit, and strange ways in courtship.

Mr Lyons does not attempt here any continuous narrative or orderly plot, but from the medley of gay talk and quick action Miss Primrose Hopper stands out with some claim to the rôle of heroine. Her roving childhood, the strange experience of a few days comradeship (purely platonic) with "the toff boy," her faithful guardian, Mr Beaky, whom actually she mothers, her resolute and pathetic loyalty to the memory of a lover for years daily expected from "Bewnezerry" till his reappearance proves him lacking in any pretence to manhood or decency; form a picture of primitive girlhood which is at once artistic and lovable. Nor, despite the death of her dream, is she destined to a sad end. Arthur's Alfred, we know, has at last won her consent, and will make her an admirable husband.

"Sixpenny Pieces" has more superficial cohesion, being approximately a full-length portrait of one man. We have here a shorthand record of the slum doctor; tales of cases, talks in the consulting-room, minutes of the daily round. This is an excellent medium for the exercise of Mr Lyons' peculiar gift for lightning sketches. We all, especially the poor, are wont to give ourselves away in talk with the family doctor, and Mr Lyons has chosen the best possible occasion for his witty impressions of these little known Londoners, the black sheep and the white. The doctor, whose fee for all cases is sixpence, has very original, but popular, methods of treatment which, just because he thoroughly understands his patients, are generally crowned with success. In reality, he is mainly concerned to divert the mind and direct will. After his own bluff manner he employs faith-healing. But, though Mr Lyons insinuates that more than half his medicines are no better than coloured water, I am myself convinced he is also an adept in the science of his profession. Morally, beneath the surface, the man is obviously no humbug. He overworks himself without stint, and cheerfully accepts the most unpleasant duties at all hours of day or night.

That weirdly precocious daughter of his, again, is a most fascinating young person, for whom any man would be proud to fetch and carry; nor can we easily forget the enthusiastic young artist in occupation of the doctor's wash-house.

They are a wonderful household, facing the stern realities with a courage that is only the more heroic because they are ever ready to laugh at the quaint surface of things; and Dr Brink appreciates the philosophy of the poor.

In " Kitchener's Chaps " I do not think Mr Lyons has chosen the best of his tributes to " the soldiers of the Queen." I seem to remember in the contemporary press, certain quite fascinating sketches of our immortal " Tommies," which I had hoped to enjoy more thoroughly in this little volume. Still, he knows his man, and here, too, throws many an attractive, quite unexpected, sidelight upon typical recruits, and some others—whose part in the Great War was not conspicuously heroic. The two " dusty old men," shut up for all time with their dusty records, are positively a revelation, the occasion for much thought—and there are others.

Moreover, Mr Lyons understands fear (which comes to many a brave fighter), and that courage which means true heroism. The merry tale of Private Blood who lost his ticket, on the other hand, is quite inimitable. " I'm the biggest fool in the battalion, I am. It's true what I'm telling you, lady, you arsk any o' my mates."

We can quite understand why Todd Pilkington, "the man who spilt the coffee over Mrs Governor, you know," quarrelled with the soldier over his pyjamas. They were alone together, up in the Bush—"It's the climate, I suppose, or the beastly mosquitoes, or rotten human nature."

In all probability the characters in "London Lot" are familiar to many of us who have never read or even heard of Mr Neil Lyons. When Mr Gerald Du Maurier produced "London Pride," its dramatised presentation, at Wyndham's Theatre, we all learnt to love Cuthbert Tunks and Miss Cherry Walters; we grew very familiar with Silverside; we were seriously disposed to kick the Mayor. And we have not yet forgotten the young costermonger of Bunter Row; nor his "parlez foreign"—"Pardon, I don't 'ear foreign, I only speaks it"; nor his "remarkable loss of memory"; nor the "remote village called Great Topleigh," where the ward-maid told him to "take orf that sore throat." Wherefore the "book of the words" must have had many readers, who have welcomed the opportunity of more intimate, and permanent, acquaintance with this delightful company of simple, good-hearted folk.

It is not essential to our purpose to go over Mr Lyons' many other amusing volumes, such as "Cottage Pie"—a country spread; "Simple Simon"—his adventures in the thistle patch; "Clara"—some Scattered Chapters in the life of a hussy; or "Moby Lane"—and the rest.

NEIL LYONS

Mr Lyons does not repeat himself, but he works always in one vein, and the same manner. What he gives us is a shrewd, penetrating, and sympathetic picture of Cockneydom; its vigorous phrasing and genial alert nature. Something akin, and yet in vivid contrast to the drab feverishness of realism. The reverse side of what his more consciously artful contemporaries have chosen to depict; in illustration of their morbid pessimism, and what they call their conviction of truth. Mr Lyons, too, calls a spade a spade, and does not shirk facts. But he can see the sunshine over the shadows, light in darkness, the merry and kind heart in the starved, stinted body—" a good deed in a naughty world."

This is a part, as we maintain not without its literary value or significance, of that intimate revelation of life as it is, with and around us to-day; which we recognise as the chief aim and intention of contemporary fiction to complete.

HOOKEY	1902
MATILDA'S MABEL	1903
ARTHUR'S	1908
SIXPENNY PIECES	1908
COTTAGE PIE	1911
CLARA	1912
SIMPLE SIMON	1913
KITCHENER'S CHAPS	1915
MOBY LANE	1916
A KISS FROM FRANCE	1916
A LONDON LOT	1919
A MARKET BUNDLE	1920

FRANK SWINNERTON

THERE are, I think, two main reasons why Mr Swinnerton stands rather apart from, and ahead of, his contemporaries.

In the first place he is frankly, and without fear of consequences, on the side of youth. He has the undimmed outlook, the crisp incisiveness, the moral and intellectual courage which belong to our entry upon life—when not warped or hampered by self-consciousness, an exaggerated missionary spirit, or the determination to pose. He is, for himself, cheerfully careless about art or culture. He is an explorer, not an iconoclast.

It is, perhaps, this wholesome independence of character which itself also produces the gifts and manner that further distinguish his work: making each novel a finished, compact achievement. One enjoys Mr Swinnerton's books largely because they are clear and short, admirably constructed, and well thought out. There is no fumbling in characterisation, no doubt about what his people stand for, no vagueness about their struggle for life. He reveals a definite object throughout, which is, in the end, achieved with success. He knows what he means and has the gift to express it.

"Nocturne," for example, recalls the finished artistry of Miss Dane's "Legend." The whole story occupies only one evening, but there is enough said. Jenny's philosophy, both of life and love, receives most ample illustration : nor are we more in doubt as to the true inwardness of her less charming, but most loyal, sister, who "wanted a home, and loving labour, and quiet evenings of pleasant occupation. To whom the daily work came with regularity, not as an intrusion or a wrong to womanhood; it was inevitable, and was regarded as inevitable." Verily Alf, sober, honest, and "a good worker at the bench," was born to be her man; though he "fancied" Jenny, and had to be pushed into happiness. They thought love, indeed, a "wonderful thing, but life simple enough." Not for them to change the order of the world.

Things were not quite so straightforward for Jenny, who found herself "outside, a misfit." All her life she had been at war with the "cowards" of this world, enemies to freedom, because they "liked the music of their manacles . . . you've all got to have one pattern, whether it suits you or not. Else you're not 'right.' 'They' don't like it." It was always "they" who mangled life for a girl: unseen presences, never clearly visualised or capable of precise identification; but none the less masters of destiny. A crude enough personification of the traditional conventions, middle-class respectability, God of her class; that which must be, because it has been from time immemorial.

> "She, indeed, had defied 'them,' gaining the freedom she so cherished as her inalienable right. . . . For her real freedom was her innocence and her desire to do right. It was not that she wanted to defy, so much as that she could bear no shackles and that she had no respect for the belief that things should be done only because they were always done, and for no other reason but that of tradition. And she feared nothing but her own merciless judgment. . . . Those who are strong enough to live alone in the world, so long as they are young and vigorous, have this rare faculty of self-judgment. It is only when they are exhausted that they turn elsewhere for judgment and pardon."

Yet she found: "Love's giving, not getting. I know that much. Love's giving yourself, wanting to give all you've got"; till in the end she gave Keith even "her freedom." To love, to be loved, "that was her sole commandment of life—how learned she knew not." Yet it did not make her "feel so tremendously happy her own self," since "he might give his love, his care, but she knew that her pride and her love must be the love and pride to submit—not Keith's."

Mr Swinnerton's contrasted sisters are most profoundly revealed in two love scenes, of which Mr Wells thus praises the first:

> "If there exists a better writing of vulgar love-making, so base, so honest, so touchingly mean, and so touchingly full of the craving for happiness, than this, I do not know of it. What a dance among china cups, what a skating over thin ice, what a tight rope

performance is achieved in this astounding chapter! A false note, one fatal line, would have ruined it all. On the one hand lay brutality; a hundred imitative louts could have written a similar chapter brutally, with the soul left out—we've loads of such ' strong stuff ' and it is nothing. On the other side was the still more dreadful fall into sentimentality, the tear of conscious tenderness, the redeeming glimpse of better things in Alf or Emmy that would at one stroke have converted their reality into a gentle masquerade. The perfection of Alf and Emmy is that at no point does a ' Nature's gentleman ' or a ' Nature's lady ' show through and demand our refined sympathy."

Of the Jenny-Keith dialogue Mr Wells, perhaps wisely, attempts no analysis, because it covers subtleties beyond summarising, that final individuality which is far truer to real humanity than any generalisings of the philosopher.

These two, indeed, are a little—only quite a little—more refined than the others; and over the four looms the majestic invention of " Pa," who " binds the bundle and makes the whole thing one " by the " enviable triumph of truth and humour." The " atmosphere " of the book " is made and completed and rounded off by Pa's beer, Pa's needs, and Pa's accident."

Mr Swinnerton, very possibly through his profound interest in youth, has adopted a rather similar foundation of contrast between a pair of sisters in at least two other novels : " The Young Idea " and " The Casement "; while it is scarcely a strain upon coincidence to claim a like emotional origin for " September," where the rôle of heroine is shared by aunt and niece.

"The Young Idea," certainly, emphasises something perilously near the loss of youth, since the interest is centred upon Hilda, in whom "contact with other people, acting upon a nature fresh and unsuspicious, but without great natural strength, had dimmed the first freshness of her love of life." But on the other hand, if the opening chapters reveal a young girl, unnaturally matured, love in the end renews her youth; and we leave her "unashamed and undoubting—for the first time aware of her power to minister and console, with no room for scruples or fear or the clamorous questionings which had hitherto prevented her from taking a clear and courageous course."

Yet it is here that Mr Swinnerton proclaims, most definitely and concisely, the Revolt of Youth. They are no longer content to leave the world in the hands of those to whom "youth was a thing to be employed for the execution of the designs of middle age." Underlying their vague unrest, their perhaps unreasonable impatience, their eager questions, their very varying demands for a new world: this, I take it, really expresses the most deep and permanent conviction of this generation. Our young men and women to-day mean to take things in their own hands, to remake life for themselves, unhampered and uncontrolled.

Wherefore, no doubt, he also emphasises in this place a danger which is only the more real for its intense pathos—the "smothering" effect of unselfish love. Eric Galbraith was bound to his mother by ties far stronger than duty. "She alone gave his life the emotional colour which, but for her, he must have found elsewhere." They were real comrades. Yet this "tied him, checked his freedom . . . had upon his character the lethargy inducing effect that a feather bed might have had upon his body." And, "slowly, the enthusiasm of the young idea was being sapped—very slowly, because it had no positive discouragement to combat : only a force more secret, more potent, incomparably more subtle." But "his ambition, unperceived, was slackening—his mother's influence was all on the side of contentment and unoriginal interests, from which his personal nature was turned, yearning for the youth's ideal of conflict and triumph."

It is the old, old story of the struggle between man's duty to himself and his duty to others : embittered, almost inevitably, by an honest conscience and true sympathy. In "The Young Idea" Eric is "set free" by his mother's death—not, of course, a final solution applicable to all cases, but it enables the author to leave his young hero and heroine on the threshold of life, as to which they have no fear, for which one may feel they are—to an unusual degree—morally ready and well equipped.

"The Casement," as we have said, also illustrates, between two sisters, the qualities that distinguish untamed youth. Olivia, the elder, had loved (romantically) one Paul Trevell, but, recognising the incompatible, turned to the more commonplace, but wholly charming Robert Burton, a thoroughly good fellow, with whom she is quite genuinely in love. Then a perverse fate leads the two men into business together and personal friendship; whereon Olivia, living over again the old days, endeavours, with innocent honesty, to feed her affections on both. "She could never admit—to herself willingly in so many words, that she loved Paul, because she was married, and because of course you could only love one man at a time."

But Loraine, clear-eyed and remorseless after the way of youth, was at once more direct and more complex. "All she wanted was to understand why everything went on, and why people lived, and made happiness outweigh disaster." Now she was "placed once and for all—in her own imagining—among the gods: for the first time in her life she was in conflict, the thing that makes poetry of life." To her it seemed "Olivia was the mystery; but Paul was the danger."

Holding her sister queen among women, passionately loyal to the good Robert, she flung herself, utterly reckless of consequences, full-tilt upon this ugly perversion of a straight moral issue. She would uphold love, as she saw it, at all costs, fight for the established order of things. But her original methods of warfare capture the fancy. Starting, naturally enough, with distrust of her sister and dislike of Paul, she rather suddenly conceives the idea of carrying war into the enemy's camp by a bold attempt to capture the man herself. For her to love and win Paul meant a clean fight. It was so simple and so fitting that she should bid for happiness.

And Mr Swinnerton fully secures our sympathy. With extraordinary skill, never obtruding its craftsmanship, he reveals Loraine quite unconsciously falling in love. The twin desires—of Paul for his own sake and to save her sister—grow side by side, strengthening each other unawares, in union to prove irresistible. It is scarcely, perhaps, a hard-won victory, since Paul, though like Olivia stirred by old memories, found Loraine's " spirit rising to his and his to hers," as no other had drawn him. It was she who " alone stretched out her hands eagerly to the future, saying, ' Come and find me.' And, far more than the others, she had courage and self-reliance to carry her onward."

Olivia, indeed, does not submit without a struggle. Perhaps the secret of her hatred of Loraine's resolve was that she could not for the life of her grant the possibility of Paul loving the two at the same time. Yet, in the end, since she knew herself to be " very happy, and very lucky and comfortable " : since " she took pride in her house, and her housekeeping, and her servants, and was glad when Robert pinched her cheek "; she accepted defeat, growing, indeed, to find happiness therein, true happiness : " It seems the most natural thing." It is natural that youth should triumph.

There is, indeed, another interesting and

original character in "The Casement":
Michael Reay, poet and amateur burglar, who
has his influence upon the others. Loving—
after a fashion—first Olivia and then Loraine,
idly confident in turn that he will win both, the
man remains absorbed throughout in the study
of his own poor egoism; now exalting, and again
in despair. Only the manly sympathy and
bracing kindness of Paul pulls him together at
last into something approximating manhood.

I doubt if Mr Swinnerton has ever achieved
quite so satisfying, and artistic, a triumph as
this finished storyette : of characters absolutely
individual, yet so ingeniously contrived for the
exposition of an idea.

The actual plot of " September " moves along
almost exactly the same lines. Marian, indeed,
has far less reason for happiness with her
husband; longer—and more bitter—experience
to stir her jealousy of youth. There are
naturally more obvious and also more essential
contrasts between her character and Cherry's;
who is, moreover, rather hard and aggressive in
her modernity—as Loraine was not.

" If Marian could have prayed for a gift, she
would have demanded joy in her life. Instead,
nature had given her, as compensation, the
strength and courage to endure her own pain,
and the ability to imagine and soften the
distress of others. If it is not the first of gifts,
it is among those most rarely bestowed upon
mortals, and is without price."

We find her, in fact, already both confidant

and mother to her somewhat primitive husband, Howard Forster; himself given to bucolic and athletic pleasures, completely outside her intellectual and moral interest. He had been, too, spasmodically unfaithful, without permanent disloyalty, and rather childishly proud of secrets he never suspected she saw through with ease. There was between them no genuine union, but quite good-humoured and tolerant companionship. Then Mr Swinnerton provides an awakening for both.

Howard is captivated, far more seriously than ever before, by his wife's niece, Cherry, who responds with a curiously hard, uncalculating abandon. Her " eyes were quite cold. They were wide open, clear and unreadable, without a trace of sin, without a trace of trustfulness." A most difficult nature, drawn with rare directness, and yet subtlety. Marian " was too experienced to expect moral standards from young women," but she recognises, of course, the terrible risk of tragedy ahead. Here is a girl to whom the ordinary, conventional appeal —the mere warning of danger—would be meaningless : who would, indeed, hotly resent an air of outraged virtue, the attempt at guidance, or even advice, from experience based on tradition. She is quite sure of herself—and of the man; scorning the calm of age and its dead passions.

And Marian, understanding, seeks only for utter confidence between them; which the other, cold and suspicious, will not give. Then to the older woman comes a hint of the great mystery.

A chance, it seems, to live in another's pure devotion, to be at last herself unafraid. The boy, Nigel Sinclair, fancies himself in love with her. His genuine sympathy, quick understanding, and unswerving loyalty, bring to her tired heart something perilously akin to the perfect union of true marriage. She is young enough, warm-hearted, with her emotion only half mastered, her susceptibilities untamed. Surely she has a right to live.

Only because she cannot forget Cherry, and will not desert her, because at the bottom she knows life has something better to give Nigel, she finds strength to resist temptation.

Wherefore, with infinite patience, unswerving courage, and a profoundly tender love, she bends her whole heart and will towards the unfolding and realisation of the natural affinity neither at first suspected between the two *young* people. Apart from the unnatural emotion that had been excited in each, and the cross-jealousies attendant thereon, there were special difficulties we cannot indicate here—in the individual temperaments of both Nigel and Cherry; but, freed at last—by Marian's heroic endeavour for its full dominion, love is justified of its children, building from youth, for all its sharp edges, the true woman and the true man.

In the mechanical process of the final adjustment, indeed, blundering Howard plays his part. At one last crisis between self and selfishness, he comes upon Marian—"Just because I'm so damned jealous, my dear," he said simply and very humbly—thereby opening a way towards better things, even for middle age.

It is not, I think, over fanciful to read into Mr Swinnerton's first novel, "The Merry Heart," a—possibly quite unconscious—apprenticeship to these four little masterpieces on Youth. The light-hearted, if somewhat whimsical, Locritus has an individuality of his own; but he may be also regarded as a sketch or study for the more finished portraiture of later novels. His mother, again, has in her the beginnings of Mrs Galbraith, while neither his friend, his sister, nor his " lady " are so assured as Cherry, Loraine and Keith. As to the elements of " gentle melodrama," finding their last word in the childlike secret of Mr Lockery senior, Mr Swinnerton handles these dangerous topics with amazingly gay dexterity, though he has never repeated the experiment.

Otherwise " The Merry Heart " foreshadows more social, and as one might say controversial, subjects on which his two most elaborate novels —as well as " Shops and Houses "—are rather carefully built up.

" The Happy Family " is, at least, in atmosphere and plot, a vigorous and unsparing disclosure of the innate vulgarity and soul deadening influences of the lower middle-class drudge, male and female. " They did not know, because it was mercifully hidden from them, that they were miserable." As Dennett, really loving his mother and sister, remarks, " The futility, the hopeless stickiness of an Amerson party seemed to make the whole family as undignified and sprawling as a cage of puppies in a dogshop, blindly pawing each other, nestling one within the other, until someone pointed a finger and said, That one please." Of the girls' lovers again, we read : " Gower was a steady, sober man of thirty years, who treated Grace rather like intelligent meat. Moggeroon was shy and elusive as any young man can be who keeps himself with difficulty, and yet has an instinctive love of dalliance." Tom, the elder brother, stands for common sense and responsibility, as they are understood in the suburbs; and Teddy's " idea of living was simply the exhaustion of time. . . . He had no power to rest, and no power to imagine."

Mr Amerson has no place in this " happy " family beyond that of wage-earner; all follow the lead, accept the standards—moral and social— of their inane mother, even while, more or less actively, resenting her interference, and for the most part furiously jealous of each other. They quarrel—noisily, and yet they stick together. There are, too, moments of sin; a threat of bankruptcy—stirring to real passion, hinting at tragedy.

All of which, naturally, depends for the effect of drama upon contrast—with the heroine. Mary, alone, was *different*. She was—cruelly— " cramped and held." There was no room for her, no chance of being alone. " She felt there was nothing in her life : that it had become something simply composed of routine, of setting breakfast in the morning, of washing dishes, of setting dinner, tea, and supper, of avoiding Grace and evading supper."

Accepting her place in life, she was no willing drudge. And, what cut far more deeply, she had no sympathy with their ideas of pleasure, no patience with their bickering or their romps, no use for their young men. There was "contempt clear in her eyes for the passion vulgar people always have for scenes."

In the wider world, the freer nature, represented by Roger Dennett, she recognises possibilities; though he—who likes, admires, and pities her—is at first attracted by the pretty, but hard, sister of one Septimus Bright; while the man Bright woos Mary. Complications arise, and Mary, just to escape the "family," engages herself to Septimus : Roger falls into disgrace at his office—through no fault of his own. Trouble, however, reveals hero and heroine to each other, and the result is happiness.

Mr Swinnerton, here, does not deal with any marked social distinctions. The superiority of the Dennetts comes from stronger personality, and slightly more fortunate surroundings, not from class difference.

In " The Chaste Wife," the contrast, or mixture, is more clearly marked; and, perhaps in consequence, the emotional crisis is more subtle. Priscilla Evandine starts life with almost everything a girl can desire. Her father, a brilliant and fascinating literary man, if not a genius; her mother, one of the most charming women we have met in fiction; her brother, a cultured enthusiast. The society at her home, all the family friends, are congenial.

Yet, not unnaturally, perhaps, she falls in love with, and soon marries, a poor relation. Stephen himself has a difficult nature, and circumstances had combined to embitter him. To begin with, he is very nearly, if not quite, a genius. Secondly, his father is an " impossible " person : given to drink, quite unprincipled, and an incorrigible, well-dressed idler, who must have his " little comforts," and expects his children to provide them. There is, too, a spoilt younger brother wanting the pleasures of life, without moral backbone to work for them. Only Dorothy, the " perfect sister," breaks the monotony of a hard life.

Stephen knew how " hunger forces men to their knees. He could not cut the painter. Life was complex." He would not seize complete happiness in marriage, at the cost of neglecting his own people. Wherefore, because he had been forced into egoism, stiffened in prejudice, he could not let Priscilla see " inside his life," and trouble grew up between them. " What you must do is unclench yourself," she tells him; but he cannot so far revolutionise his nature. Both are ready for real union and complete happiness, but neither would shirk other responsibilities. " She could not think that he was only in the world to make her happy," and desired, above all, a full share in his work. He was eager to give her the pleasures and cultivated society she had enjoyed in her parents' home.

Fate, meanwhile, is weaving for them even a greater danger. Stephen, in the old days of loneliness, had pitied, and consoled unwisely, a really charming, though empty-headed, young married woman, married unhappily. Priscilla had to acknowledge the relief of talk with one Hilary Badoureau, a rich, cultured, and quite decent friend of her brother's: a friendship which Stephen, in his humility, rather encourages than resents.

Yet, inevitably, they suffer from mutual jealousy and misunderstanding. The test of character emerges from a contrast in attitude: "On the one side reasonable acknowledgment and a strict sense of rectitude; on the other, passionate chastity of deed and thought, in no way self-righteous or exclusive, but religious in its intensity." There is a real, and profoundly emotional crisis: serious danger of final shipwreck. Mr Swinnerton, however, assigns the victory to love. He shows us how deep and sound an emotion there was between these young people, bringing trust out of doubt. Because he "loved Priscilla above all things," Stephen "kept his head." She, too, put love first. Wherefore, despair may approach, but can conquer neither; and, in the end, they win through to all the best life has to offer.

Nowhere else has Mr Swinnerton attempted so serious a study of human nature. Seldom have two fine, but no way perfect, characters been so truly revealed. " The Chaste Wife " gets very near the heart of the matter between man and woman; the essential contrast of attitude which, once bridged, will give strength to both.

" Shops and Houses " touches the fringe of an allied situation in lighter vein. It is here the man, Louis Vechanter, who was born in the purple, son and heir of the " best people " in Beckwith, " half a snob, half a socialist." This small country town, a modern Cranford, " isn't altogether a place, it's a sort of disease." It is a stifling atmosphere, self-satisfied, censorious, small-minded every way.

Here to woo means: " Three meetings, casual or planned, and afterwards eyebrows did their work." All new ideas, any moral independence, is sternly forbidden: " I know thinking makes you restless, and makes you do odd things, and that makes other people unhappy. *So it can't be right.*"

Into this home of the conventions come other Vechanters—poor relations, shopkeepers; the old people happy enough in their humility; son (and still more daughter), fiercely resentful. Louis, despite eyebrows, makes friends at once, forces his mother to call, and will not admit either difficulties or complications. Only because, at the moment, he fancies himself in love with a " typical " Beckwith young lady; the " consequences " for his girl cousin are not immediately either consoling or satisfactory.

Time and circumstances, revealing character, however, suffice to put matters right; and the tradesman's daughter proves happy enough, and every way fitted to become Mrs Louis Vechanter—out of Beckwith; helped by his generous, true-hearted mother.

" Shops and Houses " might almost be described as a quiet comedy of manners; handled with skill.

It is rather difficult to say why " Coquette " does not satisfy one in the same way as " Nocturne." It is not, of course, so unique an artistic achievement; but, apart from that, it has far more the air of being studied. No doubt Mr Swinnerton, in a sense, " got up " both stories; but he " got inside " Jenny and her sister. Sally Minto is " staged " throughout. One does not even feel that Mr Swinnerton himself quite saw over the footlights; and, in our judgment, he has nowhere else failed in the same way.

The actual craft here is once more magnificent. Mr Swinnerton has caught his atmosphere, and the persons of the tale, with unerring and sympathetic exactitude. The mingling of shrewd egotism with the emotional impulses of a child is given its full, subtle effect. Sally is always herself, and the triangle is completed in every word, with equal skill. The " hopeless " Toby and Gaga " the half-man " were, inevitably, too much for her. Neither could help. She must always " act for herself "; and yet could never make up her mind. Too genuinely simple-minded for an adventuress; too proud of her brain for a poor man's wife, she let her life drift into tragedy, managing it with a worldly wisdom beyond her years—just up to, but not past, the test. Being as " good as married " to one man, and the other's wife, produced complications she could not control. Because " her eye was all to the consequences," and " all her thoughts were anticipations," the present caught her unawares.

Had Mr Swinnerton felt this tale in his heart, and written it with love, he would have given us a great book. As it stands, the creative fire has just eluded him, and it falls definitely below his best work.

It is rather surprising, again, that Mr Swinnerton's most characteristic powers have not produced the excellence one might expect in his occasional short stories. He seems here almost too quiet, leisurely and composed; bordering, indeed, upon the trivial. They lack drama or movement. In " The Hand," certainly, he has given us, by way of atmosphere, an almost perfect supplementary miniature of the Surburbia he knows so well; and there is real charm in Penelope, while the plot has points. " The Silver Bells," too, reveals one over-mastering emotion, developed with clear consistency to its legitimate conclusion. But " Too Proud to Fight " is built to bear far more than it can carry. The descriptive analysis is overweighted; and, if the crisis has daring, it still fails either to interest or convince. Here, Mr

Swinnerton has really given us Much Ado about Nothing—only a note on blurred characters. There is, in a word, no real distinction about these tales, and were it not for the real novels, none would search out his name in the magazines.

It will be seen, then, that in all his novels Mr Swinnerton takes up a definite subject, a rounded tale; treats it with mastery, completes it, and passes on. Each is a finished work of art, what one may call a decisive act—as so few contemporary novels can be described. He has, I think, two guiding principles, or sources of inspiration—the needs, and the strength of youth; the supreme power of love. There is a depth and amplitude, recalling the classics of fiction in manner and structure, to be found in " The Chaste Wife "; while " The Happy Family " is a complete, fully developed revelation of a class—artistically drawn from strong individuality therein. These are his two " big " novels; but they are not necessarily finer or greater achievements than finished studies like " Nocturne," " The Young Idea," or " The Casement," and " September."

Everywhere, as it seems to me, Mr Swinnerton is, above all things, really a novelist, a craftsman—artist of the best traditions; thoroughly modern in outlook, atmosphere, and message; but classical in workmanship. No mere experimentalist, investigator, analyst, or observer, itching for self-expression, worried about the universe and his own soul, as are

FRANK SWINNERTON

most writers to-day. He paints human nature, not only himself.

THE MERRY HEART	1909
THE YOUNG IDEA	1910
THE CASEMENT	1911
THE HAPPY FAMILY	1912
ON THE STAIRCASE	1914
THE CHASTE WIFE	1916
NOCTURNE	1917
ON THE SURFACE	
SHOPS AND HOUSES	1918
SEPTEMBER	1919
COQUETTE	1921

DUE